AMERICA'S WILDLIFE REFUGES

LANDS OF PROMISE

TEXT BY JEANNE L. CLARK

PHOTOGRAPHY BY TOM & PAT LEESON ▪ JASON STONE ▪ GENE STONE

GRAPHIC ARTS CENTER PUBLISHING®

CARPE DIEM BOOKS®

To all those who love the wild.

— Jeanne Clark, Tom & Pat Leeson,
Gene Stone, Jason Stone

Text © MMIII by Jeanne Clark

The various photographers own copyright to their own images, as listed on page 143.
The map of wildlife refuges on page 5 was provided courtesy of the U.S. Fish & Wildlife Service.

Art decor prints are available for all photos in this book. Visit
www.leesonphoto.com for more information.

Library of Congress Cataloging-in-Publication Data

Clark, Jeanne L.
  America's wildlife refuges : lands of promise / text by Jeanne Clark ;
photography by Tom and Pat Leeson and Jason and Gene Stone.
    p. cm.
  Includes bibliographical references and index (p.).
    ISBN 1-55868-751-3 (hb : alk. paper)—ISBN 1-55868-753-X (pbk. : alk. paper)
  1. National Wildlife Refuge System (U.S.) 2. Wildlife conservation—United States.
  I. Leeson, Tom. II. Leeson, Pat. III. Title.
  QL84.2.C53 2003
  333.95'16'0973—dc22   2003016430

Copublished by
Carpe Diem Books®

503-286-0700 • www.carpediembooks.com
and

Graphic Arts Center Publishing®
An imprint of Graphic Arts Center Publishing Company
P.O. Box 10306, Portland, Oregon 97296-0306
503-226-2402 • www.gacpc.com

President: Charles M. Hopkins
Associate Publisher: Douglas A. Pfeiffer
Editorial Staff: Timothy W. Frew, Tricia Brown, Kathy Howard, Jean Bond-Slaughter
Project editor: Kirsten Leonard
Design: (Front cover) E. M. Watson, (Interior) Jean Andrews
Cartographer: Tibor G. Toth of tothgraphix.com
Production Staff: Richard L. Owsiany, Joanna Goebel
Printed in the United States of America

◁ ◁ *Bald eagle.* △ *Sandhill crane in flight.* ▷ *White-tailed deer.*

CONTENTS

Foreword

President George Washington once owned a piece of Virginia's Great Dismal Swamp. Harriet Beecher Stowe and Henry Wadsworth Longfellow each described it. The Union Camp Company logged its forests, then in 1973, donated forty-nine thousand acres to The Nature Conservancy. Uncertain they could manage it, the Conservancy passed the gift to the Fish and Wildlife Service, where it became the cornerstone of a new refuge and the beginning of a decades-long partnership between the Conservancy and refuges.

Formed in 1951, The Nature Conservancy has helped the Fish and Wildlife Service acquire nearly 250 parcels of land, which encompass almost nine hundred thousand acres and have a value exceeding $250 million. The Conservancy retains the cash reserves and expert staff to handle complex real estate transactions to assist refuges. Sometimes the Conservancy passes on a donation, and often it buys and holds properties until the Fish and Wildlife Service can raise funds to acquire them. At times, it leads negotiations for easements, sales, mineral rights, or property trades as it partners with the Fish and Wildlife Service.

Sometimes we've pursued unusual routes to ensure that land that should be a sanctuary is preserved. In North Carolina, the Conservancy encouraged a life insurance company to donate 120,000 acres along the Alligator River. The company was willing if the Internal Revenue Service would make a ruling on the land's value. Working with legislators and even the secretary of the treasury, the Conservancy arranged the needed ruling, and it was donated directly to the Fish and Wildlife Service, as a refuge, becoming the first recovery site for the endangered red wolf.

Our partnerships and shared goals span the entire country. The Conservancy helped to establish Mason Neck (Virginia) for bald eagles and Petit Manan (Maine) for seabirds. We bought land in Florida for the National Key Deer Refuge and used mitigation funds to set aside Coachella Valley as a refuge for the endangered fringe-toed lizard. We also helped create a refuge in West Virginia's Canaan Valley, saving these beautiful wetlands from becoming a ten-thousand-acre hydroelectric reservoir.

We are proud of our long association with national wildlife refuges and the dedicated people working on the ground to preserve a piece of our heritage. *America's Wildlife Refuges* celebrates the breadth and scope of the National Wildlife Refuge System, and a century of wildlife success stories that have helped set new standards for the stewardship of our nation's wildlife legacy. Savor these stunning images and enjoy these compelling stories about some of the nation's most treasured landscapes.

Steven J. McCormick
President and CEO
The Nature Conservancy

△ *An emblem of the American West, the bison was among the first species given sanctuary by the early Refuge System. Several national wildlife refuges were established in the early 1900s to provide habitat for the diminishing bison.*

From remote Pacific atolls to Maine's offshore islands, the ninety-five-million-acre National Wildlife Refuge System stretches all the way from the Aleutian Islands of Alaska to the barrier islands off the East Coast. This map shows the locations and conveys the scope of the 542 national wildlife refuges.

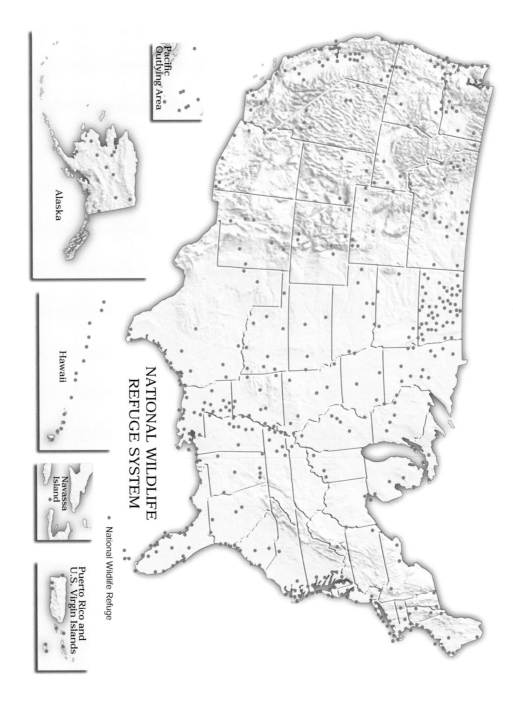

NATIONAL WILDLIFE REFUGE SYSTEM

Pacific
Outlying Area

Alaska

Hawaii

Navassa
Island

Puerto Rico and
U.S. Virgin Islands

• National Wildlife Refuge

Introduction

Imagine a system of lands bigger than the state of Montana. Envision landscapes that embrace the geography of an entire nation, from the arctic tundra and desert arroyos, to wildflower-strewn prairies and surf-battered beaches. Visualize the fish and wildlife these lands sustain . . . flocks of spiraling birds, herds of shaggy bison, runs of shimmering salmon, gatherings of velvet-winged butterflies.

For one hundred years, national wildlife refuges have preserved America's natural heritage. The National Wildlife Refuge System is the largest system of lands in the world dedicated to placing wildlife first. From .6-acre Mille Lacs National Wildlife Refuge (Minnesota) to the 19.2-million-acre Arctic National Wildlife Refuge (Alaska), 542 national wildlife refuges protect ninety-five million acres located in all fifty states and several U.S. territories. National wildlife refuges are as diverse as the character of the nation. In Florida, loggerhead turtles nest on protected beaches in the shadow of Cape Canaveral's launch pads. Weary songbirds find respite on trees in an urban New Jersey swamp. Snow geese form a sea of white on South Dakota plains and marshes. Prairie dogs inhabit burrows at a former Colorado military arsenal. Bald eagles and coastal brown bears feed undisturbed on some of the world's greatest salmon runs in Alaska. And marine life flourishes on coral reefs in the Caribbean and remote parts of the Pacific Ocean.

America's Wildlife Refuges celebrates the one-hundredth birthday of the National Wildlife Refuge System by looking at some of its resounding successes. The book's six sections include brief stories about twenty-four individual species, or groups of species. Each story showcases different refuges, where people guided by the same mission are stewards of an unrivaled system of lands focused on wildlife conservation.

In its pioneer days, the abundance of a young America seemed boundless, and so were the appetites of its people. By the early 1900s they had hunted bison and elk to near extinction, silenced generations of nesting birds to sell their showy feathers for high fashion, and drained countless marshes to farm and build their communities.

The exploitation of the nation's bounty did not go unheeded, for it also fathered far-sighted citizens and leaders, such as President Theodore Roosevelt, who nurtured the seeds of conservation and acted on the belief that America's wildlife heritage should be protected. A sportsman and a trained naturalist, President Roosevelt was as attuned to the beauty of an egret trailing its nuptial plumes in flight as he was to the seasonal pulses of migratory waterfowl. "Wild beasts and birds are by right not the property merely of the people who are alive today," he said, "but the property of unknown generations, whose belongings we have no right to squander."

He heard from concerned ornithologists, sportsmen, and others about the actions of Paul Kroegel, a slightly built, shotgun-toting boatbuilder hired by the Audubon Society to protect a struggling colony of pelicans at Pelican Island. This

mangrove island was one of their last breeding strongholds on Florida's Atlantic Coast. Roosevelt must have respected Kroegel's grit as much as he admired ethics reinforced by a double-barreled shotgun. When ornithologists appealed to the president to help the beleaguered birds, he asked, "Is there any law that will prevent me from declaring Pelican Island a federal bird reservation?" Hearing that there was none, he said, "Very well, then I so declare it," and in 1903, Theodore Roosevelt established the nation's first bird sanctuary at Pelican Island. During his tenure, he established fifty-one federal bird sanctuaries and four national game preserves managed by the Bureau of Biological Survey, giving decimated seabirds, colonial birds, bison, and other species a safe harbor. He understood endangered species before the term existed, and embraced a conservation ethic that spawned a movement, shaped a nation, and established the groundwork for what has become the National Wildlife Refuge System.

Another Roosevelt similarly responded in the 1930s, when years of devastating drought left miles of scorched fields and dried potholes that ravaged farmlands and nesting waterfowl populations throughout the northern Midwest.

President Franklin Delano Roosevelt appointed a commission of conservationists that included magazine publisher Thomas Beck, professor Aldo Leopold, and Pulitzer prize-winning political cartoonist Jay Norwood "Ding" Darling to recommend ways to restore and expand habitat for migratory birds. Following their report, and in an effort to reorganize the struggling Bureau, the President convinced Darling to take over as Bureau chief. During his fifteen-month tenure, Darling finessed millions of dollars from Congress to create new refuges for migratory birds. He also shepherded the passage of the Migratory Bird Hunting Stamp Act, or "Duck Stamp," in 1934, a one-dollar annual fee supported by sportsmen to help pay for sanctuaries, refuges, and waterfowl breeding grounds.

Darling entrusted J. Clark Salyer, a no-nonsense biologist with a flair for sensing potential wetlands and a penchant for crisscrossing the nation in his station wagon, to create the foundation of the modern refuge system. Waterfowl numbers had so plummeted that Salyer wondered, "The sturdy human stock of the prairie lands will endure. The herds will grow fat again. But can the earlier inhabitants,

the winged millions, reestablish themselves in all their early abundance?" The answer came through habitat protection, the Bureau's maturation into the Fish and Wildlife Service in 1939, and hard labor. Small staffs at fifty-three refuges built wetlands and facilities with help from Civilian Conservation Corps workers, like the young urban men who restored the burned and degraded habitat at remote Seney (Michigan) into one of the most beautiful refuges in the system. Many came with no connection to wildlife and left changed, the haunting cry of the loon leaving a whisper of the wild in their hearts forever. They helped revive the willing earth, and the wind-borne birds returned.

One such place was Mud Lake (Minnesota), a vast peat marsh coveted for farming and homesteading. In the early 1900s, promoters built more than 250 miles of ditches and spent a million dollars in an effort to dry out the wetlands, but the farming bonanza never occurred. Instead, the drying peat burned for years. The defeated homesteaders were unable to pay their drainage taxes, so the debt-ridden county sold 61,000 acres to the Federal Resettlement Administration. The troubled land was handed to the Bureau

△ *A family of river otters crosses a snow-covered pond at Red Rock Lakes National Wildlife Refuge (Montana), where two may pair up to fish in an ice hole. Lone otters often play in the water and whole families take turns tobogganing down snowy, grassy, or muddy slopes on their bellies, leaving clear evidence of their presence and their propensity for play.*

△ *The Canada goose, the most common goose in North America, nests on the isolated plains of Arctic National Wildlife Refuge. She remains prone to conceal herself among the low vegetation, occasionally raising her long neck to watch for predators.*

in 1937 to manage as a refuge for waterfowl and other species. The refuge used ditches originally built to drain the marshes instead, to carry water to revive them, and continue to use them today. Billowing smoke is now part of a prescribed burning program that, along with mowing and tree thinning, is returning nature's bounty. In 1961 the refuge was renamed Agassiz, after a prehistoric glacial lake bearing the name of a famous geologist. This remote, north country landscape is once again a haven for wildlife. Today, 125,000 waterfowl chatter songs of welcome across the fall marsh, and few refuges can rival its diversity, from moose to Eastern gray wolves, black terns to white pelicans, gregarious Franklin's gulls to secretive yellow rails.

Over the span of one hundred years, this story of stewardship, leadership, and faith has been repeated at refuges scattered across four flyways and at wild havens between and beyond. Miracles have been worked at places such as Montezuma (New York), where wetlands damaged by construction of the New York Barge Canal were restored; at Great Swamp (New Jersey), first sold by the Delaware Indians for a trifle in 1708 and finally repurchased in 1960 for over a million dollars so it could be preserved as a refuge instead of an airport; at Catahoula (Louisiana), where the scars of overlogging and overgrazing fade with the restoration of bottomland forests; and at Piedmont (Georgia), so badly eroded that the first Fish and Wildlife Service director, Ira Gabrielson, reportedly quipped that if a refuge could be made at Piedmont, one could be made anywhere.

Passage of several Endangered Species Acts, culminating in 1973, established new priorities and national wildlife refuges became a focus for the preservation of many species at risk. Fifty-six refuges have been established to rebuild populations of some of the nation's 260 listed species and the recovery of nearly one hundred species is closely tied to refuges. The Florida Key deer, Aleutian Canada goose, whooping crane, and monk seal occur almost exclusively on refuges established for them. The types of species protected also expanded. Ellicott Slough (California) protects the Santa Cruz long-toed salamander. Antioch Dunes (California) preserves remnant dune habitat in the midst of an industrial area and was the first refuge set aside for a butterfly and two imperiled plants. Lake Wales Ridge (Florida) sustains almost two dozen plants, a snake, two skinks, and a jay, all in jeopardy.

Preserving less charismatic species as part of the warp and woof of the environmental fabric parallels the evolution toward protecting entire landscapes. The purposes of many newer refuges reflect the need to preserve ecosystems and their biological diversity, from microorganisms in the soil, plants, and other living creatures to the time-wrought relationships they share. Many older refuges, such as Malheur (Oregon), have likewise expanded their original focus. All sixteen Alaskan refuges were established to protect pristine, intact ecosystems and more than half, including Arctic, Yukon Delta, Togiak, and Kenai, also safeguard unspoiled wilderness. By contrast, the challenge for refuge detective-biologists at Neal Smith (Iowa) is to rediscover how tallgrass prairie ecosystems work and recreate one of the nation's most endangered habitats. Hakalau Forest (Hawaii) is attempting to preserve and restore a lush tropical rain forest once again capable of sustaining native wildlife, including eight imperiled birds. The Akepa (honeycreeper), Akiapolau, Io (Hawaiian hawk), and others feed and breed among five-hundred-year-old koas and other venerable trees. Forest clearings and abandoned pastures now include saplings that were grown, planted, fertilized, and are tended by volunteers helping to reverse the effects of 150 years of livestock grazing. Since it was established in 1985, the refuge has built miles of fences to exclude cattle and pigs. It is fighting nonnative plants with prescribed fire, bulldozers, and hand removal, striving to restore the forest ecosystem with dozens of native plant and tree species grown in its own nursery.

This evolution from saving species to conserving entire habitats was finally recognized with passage of the National Wildlife Refuge System Improvement Act of 1997. Early refuges were few and managed individually. As migratory species slowly connected the growing number of refuges, coordination of management goals and efforts became imperative. The 1997 Act facilitated this final important linkage, describing a unique system of refuges united by a shared mission, vision, and principles for conserving ecosystems, placing the needs of fish and wildlife ahead of all uses, and assuring recreation and other refuge uses are compatible with the system's mission and each refuge's purposes. The Act links refuges as diverse as Desert (Nevada), Koyukuk (Alaska), Moosehorn (Maine), and Laguna Cartagena (Puerto Rico).

Generations of Fish and Wildlife Service employees have been guardians of this far-flung legacy. Refuge staffs now include biologists, technical systems experts, recreation planners, law enforcement agents, maintenance workers, and others using technological tools their forebears could not have imagined to face a new century's challenges, from invasive species, dwindling habitat, and the increased need for partnerships, education, and sound science, to preserving symbolic values such as wildness. A hundred years of refuge workers have nevertheless coped with the same searing heat, knifing cold, limited budgets, and long hours required to get the job done. For most the government paycheck is the second reward; the first is the chance to watch caribou return to give birth, see skeins of geese arrive at the marsh, or witness captive-bred whooping cranes reclaim the wild—and use their skills and commitment to make a difference.

It's a huge job that is being accomplished with many enduring partners. The National Audubon Society has helped

set aside scores of refuges, from Pelican Island to Pearl Harbor (Hawaii). The Nature Conservancy has made nearly 250 acquisitions to begin or expand refuges, from Great Dismal Swamp (Virginia) to Sacramento River (California). The Izaak Walton League worked for twenty years to save the largest cattail marsh in the nation and establish a refuge at Horicon (Wisconsin). Long-lasting support has also come from the Wildlife Management Institute, Ducks Unlimited, the Conservation Fund, and many others.

Hundreds of refuges have been established simply because individuals have cared. People helped turn a proposed landfill into a refuge at Nisqually (Washington); they helped save bald eagles at Mason Neck (Virginia); and together they created the first urban refuge at San Francisco Bay (California). In the early 1920s, Will Dilg, a popular sports writer, turned grief into something positive after his son drowned while the two were fishing the Upper

Mississippi River. He founded the Izaak Walton League to establish the first refuge to include fish in its purposes. From sturgeon and Higgens' pearly eye mussels to canvasbacks and bald eagles, the scope of this refuge spanning 260 miles of river is staggering. At the Upper Mississippi National Wildlife and Fish Refuge, the once-free-flowing river was tamed with twenty-six dams and locks to create a nine-foot-deep barge channel. Navigation pools and related habitats have since eroded or filled with sediment. In one of the nation's largest restoration programs, refuge staffs in four states have worked with the Corps of Engineers to transform the highly degraded habitat into islands, mudflats, and aquatic plant beds that shelter an abundance of fish and wildlife species.

Wherever they are, refuges have inspired thousands of volunteers to help with restoration, survey wildlife, lead tours, and other tasks. Volunteers helped plant more than

seven thousand seedlings at Arthur R. Marshall Loxahatchee (Florida). They exchange labor for a campsite at Pea Island (North Carolina). At Farallon (California) volunteers donate over ten thousand hours a year, assisting with everything from maintenance to surveys on this remote seabird nesting island. The versatile Turnbull (Washington) volunteers have recently logged more than fifteen thousand hours annually. Volunteers do 20 percent of the work on refuges, with an annual worth of $14 million. They often work long hours, asking for little more than appreciation and the chance to be part of the refuge stewardship.

Many take their contributions further, forming organizations of friends to help refuges. The National Wildlife Refuge Association now serves as a unifying force for two hundred forty "Friends" support groups that run bookstores at visitor centers, help with education programs, communicate with elected officials, and more. Friends groups helped

△ △ Arethusa orchids bloom in clusters at Petit Manan National Wildlife Refuge (Maine). The delicate orchid is also known as dragon's mouth, named for the yellow-tinged crest flaming down its lip. This showy orchid is imperiled in portions of northeastern United States, where it is found in protected peat bogs and wet meadows.

△ Black ducks find vital nesting and feeding habitat on a quiet marsh at Chincoteague National Wildlife Refuge (Virginia). The staff manages water on fourteen pools for its avian visitors and is replanting and grooming forests that have been attacked by southern pine beetles. More than a half million humans annually seek this popular refuge to enjoy the beach and watch wildlife, including the famous Chincoteague ponies that are descended from stock that has lived on these barrier islands for hundreds of years.

to raise funds for a visitor center at Ding Darling (Florida). They are the backbone of major events, such as the Bird Fest at Ridgefield (Washington) and the crane festival at Bosque del Apache (New Mexico). They are managing an endowment fund for state mitigation land acquired with developer fees at Stone Lakes (California).

The beauty, serenity, and spectacular wildlife gatherings at national wildlife refuges are truly a magnet for thirty-five million annual visitors. All refuges are encouraged to offer recreational opportunities compatible with refuge purposes. Sportsmen and women and their families still find a chance to fish and hunt at three hundred refuges. Children participate in environmental education programs, where young minds experience awe, wonder, and sometimes their first exposure to conservation. The vast majority of refuge visitors are people who simply come to learn, photograph, or savor wildlife in a beautiful environment. Visitors watch clouds of seabirds at Kilauea Point (Hawaii), one of the nation's most visited refuges. They witness the arrival of tens of thousands of geese at Squaw Creek (Missouri). They observe the gallant struggle of spawning salmon at Kenai (Alaska). A growing number visit urban refuges, such as Bayou Sauvage, a narrow haven for wildlife in New Orleans, and New York's Long Island refuge complex. A few follow the tattoo of the caribou's passage on a secluded trail at Tetlin (Alaska). Many come to refuges to follow paths within, to feel humbled and exhilarated, and to cherish a symbolic landscape connecting each of us to something that is both transcendent and enduring.

A century ago, President Theodore Roosevelt said that "this country of ours was not built to last a day. It is to last through the ages." The National Wildlife Refuge System, the offspring of his vision, is the living legacy of a great nation and the enduring dowry of generations to come. Take this centennial journey across continents and oceans, down well-traveled footpaths and flyways, and enjoy this opportunity to experience and celebrate a national treasure, America's national wildlife refuges. ❧

▽ *The yellow-crowned night heron's delicate crest plumes are conspicuous in the spring, during the breeding season. True to its name, this secretive heron usually seeks the cover of night, appearing only occasionally to forage along the marsh edges in the dim light of dawn and dusk. It resides year-round in the South and along the Atlantic Coast.* ▷ *No sound is more symbolic of solitude than the haunting call of the common loon. The common loon is fiercely protective, performing elaborate displays to shield its nest. Loons often carry hatchlings on their backs, though the young are able to swim when they're just two days old.*

J. N. "Ding" Darling

Jay Norwood "Ding" Darling was an avid hunter, beloved throughout the United States for his award-winning syndicated cartoons conveying strong political, conservation, and natural resource messages.

In 1934, President Franklin Delano Roosevelt convinced Darling to serve on a three-man committee to develop a program for acquiring habitat for waterfowl, then cajoled him to continue as chief of the struggling Bureau of Biological Survey. The job came with a big title, a small staff, and little money, but Darling found many allies.

When the vote for the 1934 Migratory Bird Hunting Stamp Act Darling promoted was underway in Congress, South Dakota Senator Peter Norbeck requested approval of a rider to the bill. His Swedish accent and the fact that he had left his upper dentures in the restroom made him difficult to understand, and the vote passed unanimously. The President signed the bill just before leaving on a fishing trip. His staff did not notice the rider, calling for transfer of $6 million dollars for the waterfowl program, until three weeks later. With grudging admiration President Roosevelt noted, "This fellow Darling is the only man in history who got an appropriation through Congress, past the budget, and signed by the President without anyone realizing that the Treasury had been raided."

To get the Duck Stamp program off the ground, Darling donated an illustration of two mallards landing on a wetland for the first stamp. While found guilty of continuing to plunder the nation's Treasury on behalf of refuges during his fifteen-month tenure as chief, he also refused his $8,000 salary, returning it to the government.

The J. N. Ding Darling National Wildlife Refuge on Sanibel Island, Florida, was named in his honor.

Continental Wetlands

Slender cattails and tules bend gracefully, throwing shadows across the wind-rippled water. Red-winged blackbirds retreat to nests woven between slender stalks. A labyrinth of green blades shelters broods of wary ducklings and camouflages a bittern, which sways with the undulating growth. In the space of a heartbeat, powerful wings lift thousands of tundra swans from the water, filling the sky with their flashy plumage and wild music. A momentary hush follows; then a new symphony of calls echoes over the marsh.

Across the continent, wetlands form in any basin that holds water. To the east and west, mighty North American rivers ebb and flow with the seasons, spilling over shores into extensive floodplain marshes. In the country's central frontier, wetlands form as rainfall and floodwater from swift-flowing streams fill pothole depressions scoured by centuries of glacial ice and wind. Along each coast, ocean tides bathe estuaries and lagoons, carrying a rich broth of nutrients to life in the shoreline salt marshes. Wetlands range in size from a few feet across to thousands of acres, from miles of

△ *The air vibrates with nasal calls and the whoosh of unfurling wings when thousands of snow geese join sandhill cranes and other waterfowl wintering at Bosque del Apache National Wildlife Refuge in New Mexico.*

mudflats and braided channels, carrying an ever-renewing pulse of nourishment and aquatic life. It is a cyclic world populated by pickleweed, cordgrass, algae, and other salt-loving plants that can withstand long periods of inundation beneath the salt brine. It is a place where the breeze is spiked with a rich salty tang and the music of gulls and clapper rails fills the air. Coastal wetlands are home to the fiddler crab, diamond back terrapin, harbor seal, salt marsh harvest mouse, and scores of other species that rely upon coastal rhythms for survival.

Nature's bounty is no less evident at inland freshwater marshes. Bladderwort and other deep-rooted plants populate the clear open water, sheltering fish sought by the merganser, scaup, osprey, and bald eagle. Reeds and wild rice grow in more shallow water, where long-legged shorebirds, egrets, and herons can wade and sweep their long bills to stir up a meal. Bulrush and cattails thrive in the shallows, where mallards and dabbling ducks reach below the surface to strain the water for worms and invertebrates. The mudflats bear the signatures of many visitors: the handprints of the raccoon, slide marks of the otter, a carapace imprint of the turtle, or wispy tracks of the shorebird. The marsh carries its own sharp scent, the productive smell of decay.

A cycle of passing seasons defines the freshwater wetland. During fall rain and runoff fills ponds in time for the windborne birds. Many hopscotch their way between wetlands to reach their wintering grounds. As spring green appears, marshes are recharged with rain, melting snow, and runoff and birds take to the air once again. Many work their way north, returning to their breeding grounds. Some remain to mate and raise their young. As the weather warms, the wetlands gradually contract and dry out. By midsummer, save for the permanent ponds, wetlands are barren until the cycle resumes.

Today dams and diversions, the chainsaw and the plow have changed theses natural processes. Many refuge wetlands are now highly managed by a small army of skilled workers who install pumps, build and maintain waterways, then mimic nature's cycles by pumping and adjusting water levels from fall through spring, in concert with the new arrivals. They also conduct prescribed burns, use livestock grazing to rejuvenate decadent uplands, plant crops, fight invasive plants, manage overzealous pond vegetation, and a myriad of other managment chores.

floodplain to entire coastal estuaries. They may remain for weeks or months, endure throughout the year, or wax and wane daily with the ocean tides.

Each fall, windborne birds come by the millions, banking their travel-weary wings toward the marshes north of Utah's Great Salt Lake. These lavish wetlands within the embrace of the Bear River offer the promise of food, safety, and respite from a savage northern winter. Rain and snow-melt fill the thirsty landscape, transforming sun-baked soil, laden with dormant seeds and larvae, into freshwater wetlands and mudflats.

Bear River and other wetlands help define four ancient migration corridors that connect migratory birds to their summer breeding and winter resting habitats. Programmed by instinct and navigating by the stars, each fall birds travel from the farthest reaches of Canada and Alaska to the coastal and forest-clad wetlands of the Atlantic flyway, the ice and wind-formed potholes of the Mississippi, the plains-buffered marshes of the Central, and the lush valley and shoreline wetlands of the Pacific.

These flyway wetlands are the primary reason that more than 450 refuges were established. From the sprawling Arctic National Wildlife Refuge in Alaska's wilderness to tiny Pelican Island on the Florida coast, from Upper Mississippi River refuges in the country's midsection to Hawaiian Island refuges in the Pacific, the National Wildlife Refuge System protects millions of acres of wetlands ranging in climate from the tundra to the tropics. Refuge wetlands flank all three coasts, dot outlying islands and atolls, and are scattered across the far reaches of this great nation.

The wildlife diversity at wetlands is staggering, providing breeding and wintering sites for legions of water birds and home to scores of resident species. Eighty percent of the nation's commercial fisheries reproduce in wetland waters that also sustain their young. Half of our neotropical birds find food, shelter, and a place to nest in forest-clad wetlands. And nearly half of the nation's endangered species rely upon them for some aspect of their survival.

Many of these species seek the nation's coastal salt marshes. Here the twice-daily tides flood and recede across

Marsh management has occurred since the early days of refuges. During the Dust Bowl era, J. Clark Salyer, one of the Refuge System's first employees, traveled the country using government and Duck Stamp funds to purchase land, water, and supplies to rejuvenate the country's degraded wetlands. The Refuge System grew, first protecting land and then reviving it.

Help also came to the Bear River marshes, which had been diverted to settlements and farms. Migratory waterfowl still arrived, crowding onto a few thousand acres where three and a half million succumbed to avian botulism. From tragedy bloomed hope: creative refuge workers invented the airboat to clean up the decaying birds to stop the disease, and pressure from concerned citizens helped protect Bear River as a migratory bird refuge in 1928. Restoration revived the land until 1983, when rising saltwater from the Great Salt Lake destroyed the marshes, dikes, and pumping equipment. No strangers to adversity, refuge workers moved a mountain of dirt, installed new ditches and pumps and now, when a half-million waterfowl arrive, the refuge is ready for them.

Bear River's story of wetland loss and degradation parallels many refuges, and wetlands, throughout the nation. Until the late 1780s, the area that now comprises the Lower 48 states boasted some 221 million acres of wetlands, used by migratory birds for eons. In a little over two centuries, the number has dropped to 105.5 million acres. Wetlands are still being lost at a rate of about 800 acres per day. Iowa has lost 98 percent of its prairie potholes, California has lost 91 percent of its wetlands, and 80 percent of the Upper Mississippi River watershed marshes are gone. Only Alaska's wetlands remain largely unchanged.

These losses are compelling when considering the slim margin for error. Eighty percent of the Western Hemisphere's red knots stop at Cape May National Wildlife Refuge (New Jersey). One-third of North America's canvasback population winters in the Upper Mississippi River National Wildlife and Fish Refuge (Illinois/Wisconsin). Half of the nation's duck production occurs at many rain- and snowmelt-dependent prairie pothole refuge wetlands and waterfowl production areas. Sudden drought, disease, or land use changes could mean catastrophe for these birds.

When Paul Kroegel, protector of the nation's first refuge, placed his convictions and 12-gauge shotgun between imperiled brown pelicans and armed plume hunters, he set a new standard for waterfowl and wetland protection. From the early Migratory Bird Treaties to contemporary North American Waterfowl Management Plans, from JointVentures that cross political boundaries to waterfowl, shorebird, and

△ *In North Dakota's Missouri Coteau, mixed prairie grasses encircle hundreds of pothole lakes in the heart of our nation's duck production region. Poor soils and frequent prairie fires deterred settlement, sparing much of the area from wetland drainage and the plow. More than twenty-six thousand acres are protected at Lostwood National Wildlife Refuge, where most of the wetlands are natural and almost three-fourths of the refuge is virgin prairie.*
▽ *Wetlands are among the most productive and diverse habitats on earth. A statuesque great egret remains intent on fishing in the shallows as a wary white-tailed deer traverses a secluded marsh.*

songbird alliances, the preservation of wetlands is being addressed on an international level.

Wetlands, especially refuge marshes, have found long-time champions in the National Audubon Society, The Nature Conservancy, Izaak Walton League, National Wildlife Federation, Conservation Fund, and Wildlife Management Institute. Ducks Unlimited has raised hundreds of millions of dollars for wetland conservation and become a leader in marsh restoration, often in partnership with the Fish and Wildlife Service.

In the process of saving refuge wetlands, local groups and individuals have learned that they are valuable places. They hold floodwaters and help recharge and purify groundwater supplies. They help cleanse community drinking water. They generate billions of dollars annually from commercial fishing and recreation, some supporting entire communities. They preserve stunning vistas and restore our spirits.

Whether they're called bogs, bayous, swamps, pot-holes, fens, pocosins, or vernal pools, wetlands are perhaps the most productive habitats on earth. A single wetland can sustain abundance in the millions: legions of ducks, geese, swans, and shorebirds; colonies of wading birds, cormorants, and gulls; gales of songbirds and birds of prey; herds of elk and deer; families of river otters and muskrats; packs of coyotes and foxes; and a teeming multitude of insects, amphibians, reptiles, plants, and microscopic creatures whose life processes and fates are intertwined. These creatures know only an ancient instinct, and a route that leads to renewal, relying on the promise of the enduring seasonal cycles at the nation's wetlands. ◆

△ *Their conspicuous black wing tips evident, snow geese glide in for a wetland landing. Over a million may stopover at Sand Lake National Wildlife Refuge (South Dakota). Half that many routinely visit DeSoto (Iowa) and most of Nevada's snow geese find refuge at Stillwater.* △ △ *Springs flow from the Nebraska sandhills to eleven managed pools and marshes at Lacreek National Wildlife Refuge (South Dakota). From Canada geese to pronghorn and prairie dogs, flora and fauna are diverse at this refuge overlapping eastern and western habitats.*

Forrest "Father Goose" Lee

When refuge biologists needed to develop a captive breeding program for the imperiled Aleutian Canada goose, their search brought them to Forrest Lee, a researcher at the Fish and Wildlife Service's Northern Prairie Wildlife Research Center (North Dakota). Lee is renowned for his pioneering restoration work with a cousin, the giant Canada goose. This three-foot-tall bird was once common throughout the Dakotas; however, by 1955, the wild birds had dwindled to barely 565 on four national wildlife refuges. The research center, refuges, and state fish and wildlife agencies coordinated perhaps the largest captive breeding program of the era.

Lee's team developed and documented husbandry methods, from selecting breeding stock and building holding pens to incubating eggs, managing for disease, and establishing wild flocks. Their work, combined with added protection for the giants, allowed the Dakotas population to swell to more than thirty thousand by 1982. Lee's skill and devotion earned him the affectionate nickname, "Father Goose."

Father Goose also brought wisdom and dedication to the ailing Aleutian Canada goose. Beginning in 1975, he visited historic nesting islands, helping to reestablish Alaskan breeding colonies. He taught the Alaskan goose keepers how to tend the eggs, feed chicks, raise goslings, prevent disease, and

later, how to use wild, migrating males as breeding stock to teach the next generation the migration route to California and Oregon.

The Aleutian Canada goose was delisted in 2001, but Lee's steady focus has not wavered. His decades-long correspondence with Russian and Japanese scientists led to the transfer of thirty-seven Buldir Island geese to Russia to begin a captive breeding program. Eighteen have been observed in their Japanese wintering grounds by a Lee admirer, a Japanese colleague who calls himself Son Goose. "The geese show us that boundaries between countries do not matter," says Lee, now in his eighties. "In their eyes, we are all one nation."

Geese

Pulled by instinct, powered by muscle and feather, and fueled by food foraged along the way, V formations of Canada geese take to the air across North America. The lead bird takes the brunt of the head wind, guiding adults and youngsters to the same wetlands they have visited over a lifetime of migrations. For many, their long journey ends when they pass evenly spaced silhouettes of other Canada geese—the white signs bearing a blue image of a Canada goose that mark the boundaries of national wildlife refuges. Prize-winning editorial cartoonist J. N. "Ding" Darling designed this refuge sign while he was chief of the Bureau of Biological Survey, the precursor of the modern Fish and Wildlife Service. At a time when duck and goose populations were imperiled, the sign depicting this once-common wild goose symbolized the fledgling agency's commitment to protect migratory waterfowl, a promise that is being kept today.

Families of brant from the arctic regions above Hudson Bay (Canada) skim along the Atlantic Coast from Maine to Florida, with refuge stops every few hundred miles. Sometimes nearly 125,000 of these small black geese pass the winter at Forsythe National Wildlife Refuge (New Jersey). Most of the 145,000-acre refuge is salt marsh and one of its purposes is to manage wintering habitat for the brant. One day a few hundred and the next day tens of thousands of brant arrive, a vast smoky cloud against the ocean-washed sky. The magnet for this coastal goose is the refuge's salt marsh eelgrass and sea lettuce beds, where a hungry bird can plow through the lush growth, rolling it into a bite-sized ball with its bill. Early refuge managers built fresh- and saltwater impoundments still used today to provide loafing areas for brant and other waterbirds. Stewardship also involves monitoring the effects of hunting off the refuge, research, and following new threats, such as the harm caused by crab dredging nets to eelgrass beds.

Pacific brant more than three thousand miles to the west also rely on refuges: most nest near the tide line on the Yukon Delta (Alaska). Nearly all Pacific brant stop at Izembek (Alaska) for six weeks, refueling on protected eelgrass beds. They depart all at once, with about one-fourth wintering at Dungeness (Washington) and Humboldt Bay (California).

From ebony brant to ivory snow and Ross's geese, from the three-pound "cackler" to the fourteen-pound giant Canada goose, geese depend on national wildlife refuges, waterfowl production areas, and the toil of neighboring farmers. Millions nest on Alaska's Yukon Delta, Yukon Flats, Innoko, and Koyukuk National Wildlife Refuges. Two hundred thousand Canada geese stage at Horicon (Wisconsin), the nation's largest cattail marsh, while one-tenth that number are a stunning sight on the desert marshes of Cibola (Arizona). Three refuges of the Western Oregon Complex were set aside for dusky geese and most of the world's population winter there and at neighboring Ridgefield (Washington). Giant Canada geese were brought back from the brink of extinction with research, captive breeding, and reintroductions at several Midwestern refuges. Snow geese have gone from almost rare to overabundance in some places. They form a sea of white on refuge ponds at Pea Island (North Carolina). More than four hundred thousand gather at Squaw Creek (Missouri), with often more than twice that number at Sand Lake (South Dakota) and Desoto (Iowa).

Most Pacific Flyway waterfowl, often three-quarters of a million geese and three million ducks, winter on six comanaged Sacramento refuges (California). The natural-appearing ponds are human-made and are among the most intensively managed in the nation. Prior to the gold rush, geese grazed on abundant grasses and tubers in the area's vernal pools and lakes. As 95 percent of California's wetlands were drained for agriculture and other uses, opportunistic geese and other waterfowl foraged on wheat, barley, rice, and other crops, sometimes before they were harvested. Hungry geese were so plentiful that wheat farmers employed goose herders who rode the crop rows on horseback, firing rifles to scare away the birds. Cabin herders did

their shooting from a one-room shack hauled by mules to the center of a quarter-section. Like many other refuges, Sacramento National Wildlife Refuge was established in 1937 to lure ducks and geese from neighboring farm fields. A small army of Civilian Conservation Corps workers built roads, dikes, channels, ditches, water-control structures, lakes, and ponds. In 1938 they planted eighty acres of rice and 115 acres of millet, which were completely consumed in just three nights. The planting continued for several decades, and now this refuge, like most, manages wetlands to produce a banquet of natural edibles.

From Rice Lake (Minnesota) and Crab Orchard (Illinois) to Hagerman (Texas) and Montezuma (New York), refuges across the nation farm for wildlife. Local farmers often do the growing, keeping a majority of the crop, but leaving behind a percentage for ducks and geese. Refuge staffs also work closely with neighboring farmers, ranchers, and duck club managers, offering technical assistance, granting opportunities, and more to those willing to till their soil for a nation's waterfowl legacy. A sweeping network of refuges provides sanctuary and actively nurtures these important partnerships, an act of faith to ensure that goose and duck music will fill the air and the seasons of their refuge homecoming will endure. ✔

△ Greater white-fronted geese nest within an unbroken sea of spongy tundra grasses that extend for miles. It is among four species of nesting geese at Yukon Delta National Wildlife Refuge (Alaska) that have recovered from overhunting following a management agreement between the refuge and hunting groups. The refuge is one of the most important nesting and migration corridors in North America. It sustains three-quarters of a million geese, and four hundred thousand of these are white-fronted.

△ Conservationist Aldo Leopold felt a special kinship with Canada geese, their wild voices announcing the changing seasons of the marsh. The Canada goose is common in all of the Lower 48 states and Alaska, where it is a regular visitor to most refuges in the system. Though the ochre-colored goslings can fend for themselves soon after hatching, gregarious goose families may remain together for more than a year.

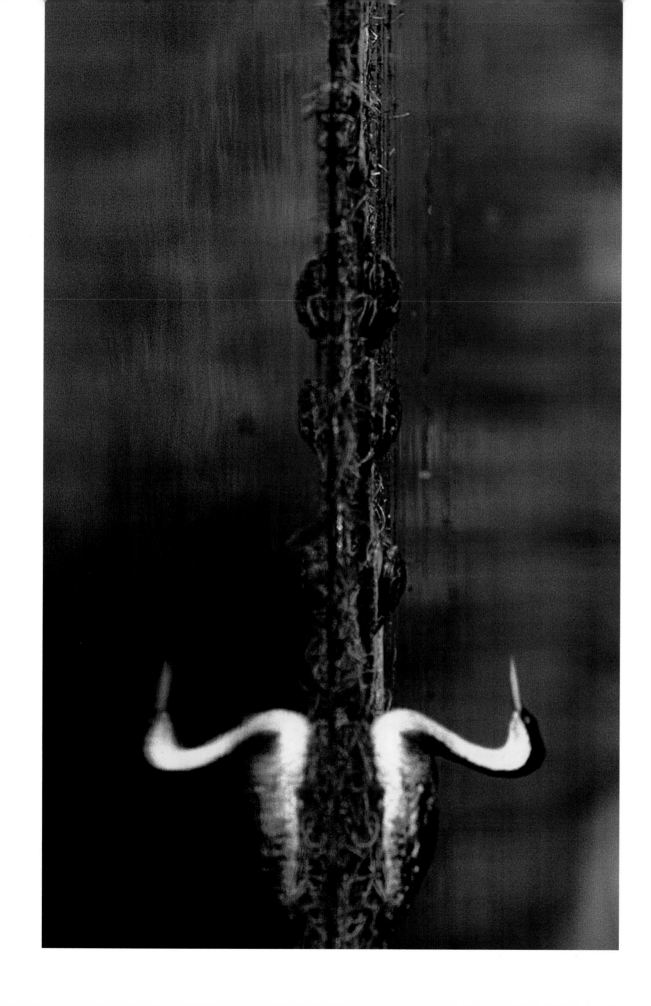

△ *The streamlined western grebe has a body designed for life in the water. It dives for fish, aided by special anatomy in its swanlike neck that allows the rapid, spearlike thrusting of its bill. Its toes are lobed, not webbed like other waterfowl, giving it better mobility underwater. Grebes often carry their hatchlings nestled in the downy feathers of their backs, the young hanging on even when the parent dives. Members of the grebe family abound at refuges as diverse as Havasu (Arizona), Agassiz (Minnesota), and Moosehorn (Maine).*

△ North America's smallest dabbling duck, the green-winged teal is one of its fastest fliers.

▷ △ The pale-colored mate of this unmistakable male wood duck nests in the cavities of old trees and in human-made nesting boxes close to ponds or streams across the nation. Her day-old young climb from the nest, often dropping directly into water for their first swim.

▷ ▽ McNary National Wildlife Refuge (Washington) sustains many of the Pacific Flyway's mallards. Over four hundred thousand visit Reelfoot (Tennessee-Kentucky) during midwinter.

Ducks

Flying in braided skeins, bunched in groups, or traveling in twos and threes, legions of mallards, northern pintails, canvasbacks, and other ducks journey south on ancestral flyways that connect their breeding and wintering homes. With them are this year's broods, tempering young wings on their first long flight as they learn the migration route between birth and adulthood.

Half of North America's waterfowl are born in the northern Midwest prairie pothole country. Even though refuges, Wildlife Production Areas, and Fish and Wildlife Service easements account for only a few percent of the region, they produce almost one-fourth of the waterfowl. J. Clark Salyer National Wildlife Refuge (North Dakota) can see over a quarter of a million birds at the end of the breeding season, and three times that many stopovers. While ice still blankets the large ponds, small potholes thaw in the warming sun, providing a bonanza of high protein vegetation to replenish the ducks' energy and fuel their courtship. Over eons of springtimes, each pothole becomes a private theater where courting males arch their necks, flick their tails, or trail a glossy wing to impress an audience of hens.

The refuge was established for waterfowl during the Dust Bowl drought. Spurred by hope and ingenuity, refuge and Civilian Conservation Corps (CCC) workers began to revive the marshes, even traveling thirty miles to find a few clumps of surviving bulrush to transplant. They re-created temporary and permanent wetlands, building ditches and structures to control rain and snowmelt they hoped would return. Generations of Salyer workers have added improvements, coped with drought or flood cycles, and handled other challenges. Their motivation was etched by hand on a cement spillway by a 1950s refuge crew—"Dedicated to a Duck."

Long before the 1997 mandate of the National Wildlife Refuge System Improvement Act, for many it was clear: refuges must place wildlife first. Waterfowl were among the Refuge System's early beneficiaries. Twice a year instinct drives these wanderers to a particular wetland or coastal marsh. Two to three million waterfowl may winter at the Klamath Basin (Oregon and California), with similar peak numbers at Sacramento Complex refuges (California). Hundreds of thousands may visit Umatilla (Oregon), Lacassine (Louisiana), and Laguna Atascosa (Texas). Two million seek Yukon Flats (Alaska), one of the highest waterfowl nesting densities in North America. Wintering waterfowl populations are also spectacular on urban wetlands at Don Edwards San Francisco Bay (California), New Orleans' Bayou Sauvage (Louisiana), and Montezuma (New York).

Thousands of wood ducks are now born at Yazoo (Mississippi) and Reelfoot (Tennessee) National Wildlife Refuges; a century ago this duck was nearly extinct. The exquisitely-colored male and his camouflaged mate nest in mature tree cavities located near water, also prime wood for homes, businesses, and other structures. In 1937, Chautauqua National Wildlife Refuge (Illinois) applied research suggesting that nest boxes might help the beleaguered ducks, designing and placing 486 bark-covered slab nesting boxes on the refuge. Following a tree-toppling hurricane, Great Meadows (Massachusetts) followed their lead and the rest is history. Nailed to trees, bolted to posts, or installed on poles twenty feet tall, nest boxes have found a home in the Refuge System and other natural areas, often constructed and maintained by scout troops and volunteers. Wood ducks now inhabit all of the Lower 48 states, num-

bering in the thousands during summer at such places as Great Swamp (New Jersey), just twenty-six miles from New York City's Times Square.

Returning and departing—this is the story of waterfowl. They do not belong to one place. They know only an instinct and a destination. They are an international treasure, relying upon a huge mosaic of wetland and upland habitats, usually purchased and restored with hunters' dollars, that span nations and political boundaries and are managed by public and private partners and conservation advocates. Waterfowl visit most of the 542 National Wildlife Refuges and more than three thousand waterfowl production areas administered by the Fish and Wildlife Service. No other single agency or organization in the world manages so much land for waterfowl, or has provided such enduring stewardship. ❧

▽ *Sometimes 350,000 canvasbacks, one-third of the continental population, gather on four navigation pools within the Upper Mississippi River National Wildlife and Fish Refuge. Protecting stretches of the river in Minnesota, Wisconsin, Illinois, and Iowa, the refuge is known for its incredible diversity, from bald eagles following the waterfowl to a mother lode of rare mussels.*

▷ *Waterfowl resting serenely at Squaw Creek National Wildlife Refuge (Missouri) captures the feeling of winter marshes across the nation. Squaw Creek maintains several thousand acres of shallow wetlands for mallards, pintail, and other visiting waterfowl, timing the delivery of water for their arrival. Its snow goose populations are legendary. This richly diverse refuge, which straddles eastern and western habitats, attracts more than three hundred types of birds and scores of other species.*

J. Clark Salyer

The early National Wildlife Refuge System was literally built from the front seat of J. Clark Salyer's personal station wagon. Armed with Ding Darling's vision of wetland refuges and $6 million from the 1934 Duck Stamp Act to buy land from Dust Bowl farmers, this talented biologist loaded his wagon with maps and gear in Washington, D.C., and was gone for months at a time. He'd look over the wounded land, meet with a farmer anxious to sell his worthless farm, and often finalize the deal over dinner, right at the kitchen table.

He thought nothing of working a twelve-hour day, sometimes driving six hundred miles over bone-jarring roads to be at a meeting the next day. To cover his vehicle expenses, the government paid him the sum of five cents a mile.

Once, after a ten-hour work day, he convinced some Washington, D.C., associates to accompany him to North Carolina's Outer Banks. The group was battered by a rainstorm, then stayed up all night at a low-class hotel discussing the potential refuge. They got stuck in the wet sand but persevered, trying to determine where the refuge should be located. The sudden sight of a mass of snow geese sitting on Pea Island's flats helped them fine-tune the new refuge's exact location.

Salyer was spontaneous, tireless, and devoted to wetland protection and restoration. During his thirty-year career, ending as Chief of the National Wildlife Refuge program, he visited all of the national wildlife refuges in the Lower 48 states. He knew them intimately, often recalling how much water was pumped at a specific refuge.

When he retired in 1964, the Refuge System had expanded from a few dozen to 279 refuges, encompassing twenty-nine million acres. One of his favorites, the Lower Souris National Wildlife Refuge in North Dakota, was renamed to honor this refuge guardian.

The Friendship of Sportsmen

Since its beginning, sportsmen and sportswomen have given their time, money, and talent to the Refuge System. The system was born because President Theodore Roosevelt, an avid sportsman, understood that ethical hunters and concerned citizens must take a stand against the slaughter of wildlife.

Dismayed by the loss of waterfowl habitat, in 1934 Bureau Chief and sportsman Ding Darling proposed and championed the passage of the Migratory Bird Hunting Stamp Act, or Duck Stamp, to raise funds to purchase and sustain wetlands. More than 635,000 hunters each paid one dollar to buy the first stamp and have continued to buy them for almost seventy years. Now fifteen dollars, federal duck stamps have raised more than half a billion dollars to purchase and sustain five

million acres in some of the most vital breeding, wintering, and migration corridors of the nation. This includes wetlands on refuges, and on nearly three thousand waterfowl production areas that protect small wetlands separate from, but usually managed by, refuges.

Individually and together, hunters and anglers have also used their time, skills, and influence to help countless refuges. Bison refuges were established with help from sportsmen and others who formed the American Bison Society. Great Meadows National Wildlife Refuge (Massachusetts) began with a donated wetland from Samuel Hoar, an avid Boston area hunter. Sportsmen lobbied to protect waterfowl at Benton Lake (Montana), renewing pressure thirty years later to assure funding for reliable water supplies. Desert (Nevada)

and Cabeza Prieta (Arizona) National Wildlife Refuges protect bighorn sheep because of help from sportsmen.

Though their support remains strong, hunters now account for only a small percentage of the thirty-five million annual refuge visitors. The majority come to learn, watch wildlife, photograph, or simply enjoy a wild place, often generating millions of dollars in tourism revenue for local communities. Ironically, refuges seldom reap the financial rewards of this nonhunting tourism, as few refuges charge entrance or other user fees. A challenge for the Refuge System during its second century will be to develop the needed financial support to serve this rapidly growing, diverse group of potential refuge friends.

△ △Wearing dazzling, iridescent breeding plumage, the male mallard is a hall-mark of the marsh during winter and spring. He is also set apart by his enthusiastic courtship dances, shaking his head and tail or swimming circles around the female to win her favor. This pageantry is not just for show, but helps a female select the best mate.

△ At one time the Columbian white-tailed deer roamed Oregon's and Washington's river valleys. It was declared endangered in 1968 because of diminished habitat, and four years later, the Columbia White-Tailed Deer Refuge (Washington) was established for a remnant surviving among the sloughs, streams, and back-waters of the Columbia River. The refuge staff periodically rounds up and relocates Roosevelt elk and controls coyote numbers to reduce pres-sure on the herd, now number-ing around 250. The refuge was later renamed to honor Washington Congresswoman Julia Butler Hansen.

△ *Mated for life, a bald eagle pair often returns to the same nest, a treetop mass of branches sometimes ten feet across, weighing up to two thousand pounds. After making needed nest repairs, they incubate two or three eggs for more than a month, and then spend the next two and a half months feeding the hungry eaglets until they can fly.*

△ △ *An adult bald eagle grabs fish in its talons, demonstrating accuracy, speed, and prowess as a hunter that earns its command of the skies.*

A superb hunter, a skillful thief, and a devoted mate, the bald eagle is one of only a few endangered species to recover, demonstrating the resiliency of nature when provided a chance, and given a refuge.

Bald Eagles

With white hood and tail feathers gleaming, the bald eagle rolls, then rides a thermal current on lazy spirals into the clouds. He planes out above the water, his seven-foot wingspan charting a flight of unrivaled beauty and easy grace. Charles Broley watched countless bald eagles command the sky, often from their own nests high in the tree canopy. The amateur naturalist and volunteer donned climbing spikes and banded eagles on Florida's Gulf coast for the National Audubon Society, often risking gusty winds and the sharp talons of returning parents. In 1939, he was banding about 150 young birds a season. A decade later there were fewer youngsters and the nests were filled with thin, shattered eggshells. By 1958, he was able to find and band only a single eaglet.

Documenting nest failure after failure, Charles Broley observed what Rachel Carson later detailed in her 1962 book *Silent Spring*: pesticides and heavy metals were destroyers of ecosystems and the causes of reproductive failure in bald eagles and scores of other species. Chosen as the symbol of our young nation in 1782, this monarch of the skies was now slaughtered and poisoned. Their numbers plummeted from perhaps 200,000 nesting pairs to fewer than 450 nesting pairs in the 1960s throughout the Lower 48 states.

The bans on DDT and other chemicals and protection under the Endangered Species Act helped lay the groundwork for recovery. In the 1970s, Virginia scientists found a single pair of nesting bald eagles. Hope drove private citizens and The Nature Conservancy to safeguard six thousand acres of resting, feeding, and roosting habitat as Mason Neck National Wildlife Refuge, the first refuge in the system devoted to protecting bald eagles and a place where eagles again nest today.

Wildlife professionals and concerned citizens made a similar stand at the Klamath Basin National Wildlife Refuge in Oregon. At one time, likely more than a thousand bald eagles overwintered in the basin, but by the 1960s, only twenty nesting pairs could be found.

Ralph Opps, a veteran eagle observer and biologist for the Oregon Department of Fish and Wildlife, made a stunning discovery about the significance of night roosting areas. Every evening eagles gathered on northeast-facing slopes in old-growth stands that protected them from wind, and offered safety and open branches to accommodate dozens of birds with six- to eight-foot wingspans.

Opps located the largest of their night roosts in 1976, a one-thousand-acre core area used by up to six hundred eagles. He and staff from Klamath Basin National Wildlife Refuge convinced The Nature Conservancy to purchase and hold the core area and another 3,200 acres surrounding it until the Fish and Wildlife Service could raise funds to buy the land. This occurred in 1978, and Bear Valley National Wildlife Refuge became the first refuge established to protect night roosting habitat for the bald eagle. Today, up to one thousand bald eagles use the basin, forming

the largest wintering concentration of bald eagles in the Lower 48 states.

Each winter of the 1980s, the refuge staff at Sequoyah National Wildlife Refuge (Oklahoma) observed a few eagles somersault through the air and lock talons during courtship displays, then carry branches to a nest the birds never used. Even though partnerships were uncommon at the time, the refuge enthusiastically responded when the George M. Sutton Avian Research Center of Oklahoma asked them to build an elevated platform, called a hacking tower, to house some of the center's progeny. For several months, they provided fresh fish to the maturing youngsters. They also gave housing and equipment to volunteers who helped monitor forty-nine eagles released on the refuge over a six-year period. Banded birds from Sequoyah are now routinely sighted in other states, and it is not unusual to see more than a dozen eagles brooding their eggs on the refuge, even through spring snowstorms. The successful partnership with the refuge allowed the center to expand its program, eventually releasing 275 bald eagles in five southern states to spur their recovery.

Dozens of refuges have been established for bald eagles, which now winter or nest at about 350 national wildlife refuges and other natural areas across the continent. Hundreds feast on fish and waterfowl at refuges strung along the Mississippi River. Huge concentrations gather at Blackwater (Maryland). They feed on fish frozen in oxbows of the Rio Grande at Alamosa/Monte Vista (Colorado) and are a common sight at Karl E. Mundt (South Dakota), another night roost sanctuary protected through a community's sale of endangered species drinking cups. They have never been imperiled in Alaska, where a thousand or more mingle in huge gatherings as they follow the spawning salmon at Kodiak National Wildlife Refuge.

The Fish and Wildlife Service upgraded the bald eagle from endangered to threatened over its entire range in 1995. Delisting is on the horizon. A superb hunter, a skillful thief, and a devoted mate, the bald eagle is one of only a few endangered species to recover, demonstrating the resiliency of nature when provided a chance, and given a refuge. ❧

▽ Whooping cranes are one of the Refuge System's newest success stories. The endangered birds began a slow comeback at Aransas National Wildlife Refuge (Texas), which protected habitat and provided adults for a captive breeding program at the Patuxent Wildlife Research Center (Maryland). Before they even hatch, captive chicks hear recordings of the parent's brooding call and the sounds of an ultralight aircraft. The chicks are raised in pens designed to simulate natural habitat by costumed handlers and make their first tentative flights behind a crane-colored ultralight. After much conditioning, ultralights are used to teach them the 1,250-mile migration route between their summer refuge home at Necedah (Wisconsin) and winter habitat at Chassahowitzka (Florida).
▷ A whooping crane at Aransas National Wildlife Refuge (Texas) feasts on a blue crab, one of their favorite foods.

Whooping Cranes

Two whooping cranes looked up with startled yellow eyes as the deep quiet of their pond was broken by a whirring sound. Stiff-legged, they urged their solitary chick into the safety of some tall sedges as a helicopter en route to a forest fire passed, then circled back to give the pilot a second look. It would seem that the tallest bird in North America, an elegant white bird standing five feet with black wingtips and a red crown, would be hard to lose, but not a single nesting whooping crane had been seen for over a decade. The future changed in June 1954, when their secluded nesting habitat was finally discovered at Canada's Wood Buffalo National Park.

Shooting, disease, and loss of their wetland and prairie habitat had caused North American whooping crane numbers to plummet to near extinction. Their only hope for survival was a struggling flock of about eighteen birds protected in 1937, when their winter home was preserved as Aransas National Wildlife Refuge (Texas). Protection has not spared these imperiled cranes from a continuing onslaught of problems. In the 1940s, the Army Corps of Engineers constructed the Gulf Intercoastal Waterway bisecting the refuge. Piles of dredge spoils buried close to 1,200 acres of crane roosting habitat and waves from barges and boats eroded several more acres per year. Protection under the Endangered Species Acts of 1966 and 1973 stopped the Corps from piling dredge spoils on the refuge but the acts did not deal with the erosion, which became severe.

By the 1990s, the slowly increasing crane population had captured the hearts of local citizens and conservation groups. Each year they visited the refuge and climbed on tour boats to watch pairs mated for life bow their heads, flap their wings, dance on air, and bugle affectionately for their partner. Guided by the refuge and Corps, a local business donated tons of material and hundreds of citizens provided labor to begin

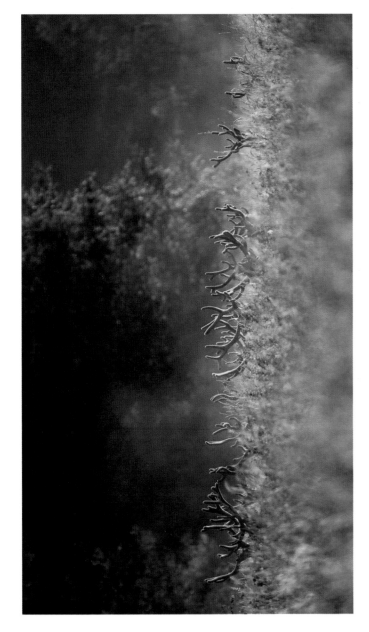

▽ *Roosevelt elk bulls are common at Julia Butler Hansen (Washington) and Willapa (Oregon) National Wildlife Refuges. A sea of antlers covered in velvet, is the only hint that this herd of bulls has bedded down for a rest. The velvet nourishes the growing antler, dries up, and is polished off on trees or fence posts.*

▽ *Tule elk are native only to California. Bulls wading in the tule marshes at San Luis National Wildlife Refuge demonstrate an association with this once-common valley habitat that is likely responsible for their name. Refuge protection and management have produced surpluses for relocation, helping the state of California reestablish tule elk herds throughout their historic range. An elevated platform offers choice wildlife viewing of sparring bulls, complete with loud bugling and clacking antlers.*

protecting the receding shoreline. A National Audubon Society lawsuit finally yielded a permanent solution from the Corps, which armored over twenty miles designated as critical crane habitat. Their dredge spoils are now being used to advantage to create new marshes. Although there are currently 185 cranes, Aransas cannot guarantee their safety. The birds remain vulnerable to hurricanes and spills of toxic products transported on the waterway. A dam has recently been proposed that will affect freshwater flows to the wetlands just upstream of the refuge.

The discovery of their Canadian nesting habitat and cooperation on an international scale has offered many possibilities for addressing these realities. Over many years scientists have cautiously removed one of two eggs produced by the nesting birds to form the foundation of a captive breeding and reintroduction program, first at Patuxent Wildlife Research Center (managed by the Fish and Wildlife Service until 1996) and later at the International Crane Foundation (Wisconsin) and Calgary Zoo (Canada). A fourteen-year effort to create a new migratory flock at Grays Lake National Wildlife Refuge (Idaho) ultimately failed, but a nonmigratory flock started on Florida's Kissimmee Prairie in 1993 is slowly increasing, providing insurance against catastrophe. Another migratory flock was essential, but how could these inexperienced birds learn the migration route?

Serendipity provided the answer when an ultralight pilot sailing on wind was followed by a skein of flying geese. From this, Operation Migration was born and eventually, the Whooping Crane Eastern Partnership, an international alliance of agencies, foundations, researchers, private landowners, and others devoted to crane recovery. They agreed to establish a flock of cranes at Necedah National Wildlife Refuge (Wisconsin) and teach them the migration route to Florida's Chassahowitzka National Wildlife Refuge using ultralight aircraft.

In the fall of 2001, eight young whooping cranes at Necedah, conditioned to the ultralight even before birth, took to the skies accompanied by three ultralights and a Cessna. They followed a predetermined route involving other refuges, twenty state agencies, and thirty-four private landowners who agreed to allow overnight stays on their property. They were followed by an on-the-ground entourage of recreational vehicles, veterinarians, and handlers. Success required decent weather—and hope. After 1,250 miles, twenty-seven stops, and forty-eight days of travel, an ultralight followed by stately white birds glided past a shopping mall where two thousand onlookers watched in awed silence, then skimmed over the palms and cypress of their winter home at Chassahowitzka. These travelers made history, and repeated it when confident wings carried them to Necedah on their own. In fall 2002 they returned to Chassahowitzka, parachuting on thermals in just nine days. They returned to a refuge with expanded wetlands, and an enlarged pen for sixteen more whooping cranes, which flew into history on the second ultralight migration.

Chassahowitzka, Necedah, Aransas—three national wildlife refuges at the heart of a conservation milestone. When President Theodore Roosevelt established the first refuges, partnership was a foreign concept and conservation was a fledgling idea. The whooping crane recovery effort is a remarkable story of ingenuity and cooperation, a fitting "poster child" for the conservation ethic President Roosevelt espoused and envisioned. ⚘

California Tule Elk

The tule elk bull shook his magnificent antlers and ground his teeth, unaware that he was profiled in the crosshairs of a .50-caliber rifle. The rifle went off, hitting the bull squarely. The stunned animal ran thirty yards, staggered, and fell, while a small group of onlookers cheered. This was the eighteenth elk, the last one. They approached their quarry cautiously. He was still alert.

In another century, this might have been market shooters bagging some of the last native elk living in the tule marshes of California's Central Valley. Instead, this was a group of California Department of Fish and Game employees, and these eighteen elk weren't dead; they were captive elk at the San Diego Wild Animal Park that had been tranquilized for their trip to a new home.

Before the 1820s, some five hundred thousand tule elk grew fat in California valley wetlands, grasslands, and oak savannahs. Early explorers compared their numbers to the nation's bison, with as many as two thousand in a single San Joaquin Valley herd.

Then gold called people westward. Annual grasses replaced native vegetation, livestock proliferated, market shooters exterminated vast herds, and tule marshes were drained for agriculture, spelling death for this unique race of elk.

In 1863 an employee of cattle baron Henry Miller was stunned to see a pair of tule elk standing in a marsh. He brought back the news to Miller, who created a sanctuary for what many believe were the last two tule elk in existence. Under Miller's protection, elk numbers grew to the point that they were damaging habitat and trampling fences, and a number of relocations took place. Most of the relocations failed and their numbers remained extremely low. Finally, in 1971, the state of California passed legislation that

protected the elk and charged the Department of Fish and Game to lead a recovery effort.

The U.S. Fish and Wildlife Service has a long tradition of working with other agencies to recover threatened and endangered species. In response to the state's request, the staff at San Luis National Wildlife Refuge in Los Banos agreed to provide a sanctuary, convert the plan's many skeptics, and cope with the challenges of managing a captive population.

In 1974, the eighteen tule elk from San Diego's Wild Animal Park were brought to a new, 760-acre fenced enclosure within the refuge's historic elk habitat. This first transfer, followed by a second in 1978, began a decades-long history of cooperation and a new chance for the tule elk.

To keep pace with the needs of the growing elk herd, the refuge improved their water delivery system, creating individual wetlands in the enclosure that not only benefitted the elk, but also a million ducks, geese, and wading birds. Prescribed burns eliminated overgrown vegetation and reestablished the grassland habitat. A public viewing platform and interpretive materials helped tell the elk story.

With good food and sanctuary, the herd rapidly increased, leading to periodic roundups every few years both to prevent overcrowding at San Luis and to use surplus elk to help reestablish new herds within their historic California range. The refuge provides hands-on assistance and support during each capture and has worked with the state on a variety of capture methods and studies. Contraceptive devices have recently been implanted in a number of cows remaining at the refuge to slow the captive herd's growth.

There are now 3,700 tule elk in twenty-two thriving California herds. San Luis National Wildlife Refuge has provided about 200 elk for relocation and these have produced hundreds of offspring. There are few places in California offering closeup views of this elk of the tules, but visitors at San Luis are regularly treated to the clamor of squeals and bugles, the sight of cows and their spotted calves, and the magnificent spectacle of these titans sparring in their native landscape. Many national wildlife refuges sustain the nation's Roosevelt and Rocky Mountain elk legacy. Only one exists for tule elk, a single refuge that has made a difference. ❧

34

△ Beavers build dams and lodges in narrow streams, marshes, and ponds to create a protective moat that discourages predators. Nature's loggers have formidable incisors that can cut through trees several feet in diameter. Their engineering activities often create ribbons of shallow wetlands that team with aquatic life and enrich the soil when the marshes dry out.

△ To regulate their temperature, turtles rely on nature. Painted turtles bask in the sun on a log to rouse their cool, lethargic bodies, especially in the morning. When they become too warm or sense danger, they slip into the water, disappearing completely except for a small wake made by their exposed nostrils.

Islands, Beaches, & Estuaries

O cean tides bathe the edges of the continent, forming an elusive, changing boundary. The life-sustaining surge ebbs and flows across estuary tidal flats and sandy beaches, leaving scalloped patterns in the sand as it retreats. It covers and exposes rockbound tide pools. It batters cliff-backed shores. Over the millennia, a steady procession of waves has severed cliffs from their land moorings to form rugged sea stacks, pillars, and islands, the offshore remnants of a former shoreline. These outcrops stand like dark sentinels, streaked by white guano (droppings) — testimony to the generations of seabirds that abide here. Offshore, an undersea world of fish and other marine creatures flourish in the shadow of undulating kelp forests and in openings within tropical coral reefs. Biodiversity is rich where land meets the restless sea, where forces that destroy also bring renewal.

In 1903, lifelong friends and photographers William Finley and Herman Bohlman loaded camping and camera gear for a trip to photograph seabirds at Three Arch Rocks off the Oregon Coast. The two wanted to document the rich seabird life before they were

△ *The remote rocks and spires of Farallon National Wildlife Refuge, twenty-eight miles off the California coast, provide welcome respite to a quarter of a million nesting seabirds, such as common murres, on the left, and the Brandt's cormorants, on the right.*

obliterated by people shooting at them from passing boats. The men braved punishing seas to reach the island and captured on film the rare and rugged beauty of these rocks and their avian inhabitants. A few years later Finley's admirer and friend, President Theodore Roosevelt, gazed in wonder at the intrepid seabirds on these sea-lashed rocks. Recognizing their value, in 1907 he declared Three Arch Rocks the first bird sanctuary in the West.

Today Three Arch Rocks is one of six refuges scattered along 320 miles of sculpted Oregon coastline. The sea stacks, reefs, and islands of the Oregon Coastal National Wildlife Refuges are an oasis for seals, sea lions, and over a million seabirds. More than 65 percent of common murres nesting south of Alaska are found largely on the Oregon Coast refuges. These long-lived birds, faithful to each other and their nesting sites, are vulnerable to disturbance during nesting season. Management includes air and boat patrols, and educational efforts designed to reach boaters, anglers, pilots, and others. Informational posters recently placed at Oregon ports and other coastal locations yielded immediate reports of wildlife harassment, which the refuge was able to quell. The refuge has also partnered with the Coast Guard and provided in-flight training regarding minimum flight distances from the nesting colonies, shared wildlife species information, and in return, is receiving help with surveillance.

Coast Guard presence also aided terns on Petit Manan Island. Now one of the largest nesting seabird colonies on the rugged Maine coast, its Arctic, common, and roseate terns and other seabirds were nearly decimated by egg and plume collectors a century ago. They began rebounding, but again declined in the 1930s due to habitat loss and growing numbers of herring and great black-backed gulls that commandeered the best nesting sites and preyed upon terns and their young. The Fish and Wildlife Service acquired Petit Manan from the Coast Guard and established the refuge in 1974. After people left the island, the larger and more aggressive gulls proliferated, nearly excluding the terns in less than a decade. By 1977, barely five thousand nesting pairs of terns remained in the Gulf of Maine, motivating the refuge and several international, state, and private partners to make seabird restoration a priority. For a quarter of a century the partners and volunteers have harassed or eliminated

the competing gulls on more than a dozen islands, sometimes following up with tern decoys and sound recordings to lure back the nesting birds. The increasing numbers of terns gliding in graceful flight, hovering buoyantly, and knifing into the surf after fish speak volumes for these concerted efforts.

As waves forge past these craggy seabird outposts, they carry a churning load of sand gleaned from battered rock and distant beaches. A weakened wave drops some of its burden on the beach while another, full of momentum, grabs sand as it retreats. Beaches continually expand and contract, washed by tides that surrender strands of kelp, crabs, and other edibles for legions of pecking and probing shorebirds.

This bounty and the safety of isolation attract piping plovers to Monomoy National Wildlife Refuge (Massachusetts), where sand and barrier islands stretch for eight miles along the Atlantic Coast. Mated pairs call to each other with clear mellow whistles and both brood tiny

▽ For over a half century the historic lighthouse at Kilauea Point National Wildlife Refuge warned sailors of Kauai's rugged coast. Today, these cliff walls and plateaus are among the few places in the main Hawaiian Islands that support nesting seabirds because they are protected by the refuge, which has fenced out dogs and routinely traps cats and other predators. Even Laysan albatross began nesting here after the 1970s.
▷ Ocean tides flood oxbow sloughs fringed with saltwater cordgrass at Rachel Carson National Wildlife Refuge (Maine), named for the famed environmentalist and former Fish and Wildlife Service biologist/editor who brought the science and magic of the sea to life for many Americans. Wading birds stalk the extensive salt marshes, and shorebirds prowl mudflats exposed at low tide.

Rachel Carson

The Chief of the Biology Division of the Bureau of Fisheries was desperate. He needed a writer who knew marine biology to produce radio broadcast scripts for a series called *Romance Under the Waters*. That summer of 1935, a quiet, determined woman happened to stop by the office. He'd never seen her writing but felt he could take a chance, and hired her part-time on the spot. He, and later the world, learned that Rachel Carson was as passionate about science as she was about awakening a sense of wonder in people with her vivid descriptions of the natural world.

Most people remember Carson for her engaging trilogy of books about the sea, or as the renowned author of *Silent Spring*, a courageous book documenting the harmful effects of pesticides on nature. Much of the material for these books came from her career (1936–1952) with the Fish and Wildlife Service as a biologist and later, as chief editor of the agency's publications. Both her scientific research and writing embraced national wildlife refuges. Her bulletins, articles, and brochures set a new standard for government writing. With the publication of *Silent Spring* in 1962, they also galvanized the world, shaping conservation

and environmental policy for the twentieth century. During an era when female scientists were a rarity, she never hesitated to plunge into the environment she so loved, whether to stand for hours in a frigid Maine tidepool, examining its rich marine life with a hand lens, ride a clattering glades buggy into the Everglades to study its life, or brave raw winter weather to watch migrating hawks that "came like brown leaves drifting in the wind." Carson wrote with the authority of a scientist and the voice of an artist, armored with moral courage and an unfailing ability to capture the beauty of the living world.

speckled eggs placed in a sandy scrape above the high tide. Monomoy is a designated Wilderness Area, so many activities that could disturb the nesting birds are restricted. Much like Petit Manan, shorebird and seabird chicks barely the size of a cotton ball were preyed upon by increasing numbers of herring and great black-backed gulls. The refuge has also culled some of these aerial raiders, creating a gull-free zone that has helped endangered plovers, roseate terns, and other species. From willets that use long bills to mine the beaches for invertebrates to short-billed dowitchers that feast on horseshoe crab eggs, this is a major Western Hemisphere stopover for shorebirds that have nested in the Arctic. The refuge hosts the second-largest nesting colony of common terns on the East Coast and serves as a major haul-out site for gray seals. Even imperiled northeastern beach tiger beetles, once common along the Atlantic Coast, were relocated here and are gaining ground.

Dozens of refuges are vital to marine life. Shorebirds gather by the hundreds of thousands at Selawik (Alaska), Cape May (New Jersey), Willapa (Washington), and San Francisco Bay (California). More than fifty million seabirds nest in huge colonies on some of the 2,500 islands, headlands, spires, and reefs within Alaska Maritime, and within the 1,100-mile-long chain of remote islands in the Hawaiian Archipelago. Sea turtles cautiously bury their eggs on protected beaches at Cape Romain (South Carolina) and Archie Carr (Florida). Tropical Caribbean refuges (Puerto Rico and U.S. Virgin Islands) that were once bombing ranges and surveillance posts now support tropic birds, seabird colonies, sea turtle nesting beaches and, with the recent addition of three-hundred-thousand-acre Navassa Island, an underwater universe of living coral reefs.

Rachel Carson, a marine biologist and prolific author who worked for the Fish and Wildlife Service for many years, considered this briny realm where life first began one of the most productive and biologically rich ecosystems on earth. It is a place where change is constant, and where the eternal rhythms of the mother sea endure. 🐚

▷ A Brandt's cormorant, identified by buff-colored feathers at her throat, nests in tightly packed colonies along the Pacific Coast.

▷ ▷ Also Pacific Coast residents, courting pigeon guillemots trill and move their bills during a nesting display.

The wind can be fierce and relentless, the storms are savage,

and the remoteness can be staggering . . .

conditions custom-made for seabirds.

Seabirds

The wind can be fierce and relentless, the storms are savage, and the remoteness can be staggering . . . conditions custom-made for seabirds. Pelagic birds live most of their life at sea, some touching land only to breed and raise their young. Their breeding and nesting is a noisy drama on a barren, rocky outpost or sun-washed tropical beach seldom played to a human audience. They usually nest in some of the most remote places on earth, gathering in huge colonies that offer protection from predators.

In a matter of days a nearly deserted island in Alaska's Aleutian Islands becomes a multistoried colony of possessive, jostling seabirds jammed into every available nesting nook. Tufted puffins with wispy plumes peek out from a platform entrance to their earthen burrows. Common murres nest on the open cliff face. Small auklets and petrels claim a narrow tunnel, moving under the cover of darkness. The clamor of barnyard calls is deafening. Long moos. Winsome whinnies. Deep moans. Piercing whistles.

Alaska's seabird population matches the state's penchant for size and grandeur. Fifty million seabirds nest in Alaska, some fifty-five species, encompassing half of North America's population; a single national wildlife refuge, Alaska Maritime, sustains forty million of them. The scope of this refuge, the most far-reaching in the Refuge System, is staggering. If superimposed over a map of the Lower 48, this 1,100-mile archipelago of 2,500 islands would arc from California to Georgia and north to Minnesota. The refuge's five units compete with each other for superlatives. The world's biggest fulmar colony, sometimes a million birds, is found on Chagulak Island. Some islands sustain the world's biggest fulmar colonies, several exceeding a half million birds. No fewer than three million crested and least auklet colonies are on Kiska, where the largest colonies on earth look like swirling smoke as they arrive and depart. Eighty percent of the world's red-legged kittiwakes nest on St. George. Birds considered rare elsewhere are common here, from tiny whiskered auklets to red-faced cormorants.

It is a gift to the world that this refuge was established to protect migratory birds, marine mammals, and the incredible habitat upon which they depend. This sprawling legacy and its demanding conditions make it a challenge to manage. While oil spills, pollution, and global climate loom as constant threats, invasive species are a grave present concern. Fur traders, bird hunters, shipwrecks, and wartime occupants brought nonnative foxes, rats, insects, and exotic plants to the islands. Fox eradication programs have been in place for decades, removing a major source of bird predation. Rats are an even more insidious curse and are now on a dozen nesting islands. The refuge has started a major trapping program and inaugurated a shipwreck strike team to deter new escapees. They have initiated studies in the Kiska auklet colonies, where rats are able to reach in small burrows and crevices that defied the foxes, and are devastating the nesters. In boats, on land, and by air, they constantly study this watery domain, noting everything from huge gatherings of fulmars to small clusters of Laysan albatross.

The Laysan albatross are often nesting parents from Midway Atoll in Hawaii, which have traveled nearly 2,000 miles to the Aleutians to catch a feast of rich oil-laden fish for their growing youngsters. Fourteen million seabirds gather in the remote Hawaiian Archipelago on sandy, low-lying islands and atolls so small they rarely appear on maps, but so extensive they stretch over 1,100 miles. Nesting birds crowd into colonies within the northwestern Hawaiian Islands National Wildlife Refuge, one of the earliest refuges established in the West to protect the overhunted seabirds. Together they support the largest populations in the world of Laysan and black-footed albatross, Christmas shearwaters, Bonin's and Bulwer's petrels, and Tristam's storm petrels, and huge gatherings of a dozen other species. Local lore is steeped with seabird stories. First Hawaiians believed the god Kane could assume the form of an albatross, and viewed the iwi, or great frigate bird, as a symbolic ancestor.

As in Alaska, generations of refuge workers are coping with introduced rats, weeds, and other unwanted intruders that have ravaged native ecosystems. Rats on several islands have required intense surveillance and eradication programs. Early refuge workers killed thousands of introduced rabbits that decimated Laysan native vegetation and drove the island's native duck and finch to near extinction. The Laysan duck and finch have rebounded, and the battle has now shifted to eliminating nonnative vegetation that displaces native plants used for nesting by two million seabirds, including the world's largest gathering of black-footed albatross. Since 1991 refuge workers, traveling huge distances and wearing clothes sanitized of seeds, have used picks and shovels, burning, and herbicide spraying, at a cost of nearly a million dollars, to eliminate common sandbur, the worst invader. By 1998 few sandbur seedlings remained and native grasses were returning, a small victory requiring ongoing vigilance often repeated on other infested islands. Safeguarding this island paradise requires a large array of tools, from coping with the massive wartime alteration of Midway Atoll to smaller projects, such as erecting nesting box "condos" for Bulwer's petrels that fly like bats and woof like dogs.

While the nation's seabird legacy is largely on Alaskan and Pacific remote island refuges, significant gatherings also occur at Petit Manan (Maine), Oregon Coastal Refuges,

and Farallon. Located twenty-eight miles from California's Golden Gate Bridge, dense fog, pummeling storms, and treacherous seas create a sanctuary at Farallon that is a world apart. The Spanish name describes clusters of rocky promontories rising from the sea, where five marine mammals and a quarter of a million seabirds gather to nest, including the world's largest breeding colonies of ashy storm petrels, Brandt's cormorants, and western gulls. This highly prized habitat was declared a refuge in 1909, and a marine sanctuary years later. Its thirteen species of seabirds and other dwellers are among the most intensely studied in the nation. The refuge has nurtured a unique thirty-year partnership with the nearby Point Reyes Bird Observatory and an incredible cadre of volunteers to maintain aging island facilities and help with monitoring.

To protect the nesting birds the refuge has removed generations of feral cats and rabbits released by former island occupants, and is now eliminating nonnative vegetation that covers nesting burrows and displaces native vegetation. Whale, seal, and seabird watching are a popular tour boat activity, so vigilant boat patrols enforce sanctuary access restrictions and boat speed limits. Volunteers are the heart of this unique refuge effort, donating more than ten thousand hours a year. Dedicated helpers brave the often choppy six-hour ride and live on the island a few days to help with everything from installing solar panels and making plumbing repairs to skippering regular boat runs to haul supplies. Volunteers here and at other refuges give richly and require little in thanks. Often their reward is the chance to hear the excited buzz of the colony or watch a tiny flightless chick run a gauntlet of poking beaks, then tumble over cliff ledges into the sea for a first swim with its waiting father. ✍

William Finley

When the Finley family relocated from California to Oregon in 1887, the providential move placed eleven-year-old William next door to Herman Bohlman. The young Bohlman and Finley shared an interest in collecting skins, eggs, and even specimens of then-rare birds. Eventually, they seized cameras and embarked upon a career of wildlife photography, creating stirring images that brought the first national wildlife refuges to the West.

The two partners thought nothing of hauling their bulky cameras, tripods, heavy glass plates, and developing chemicals on arduous and dangerous trips, such as those they made to Three Arch Rocks on Oregon's coast in 1903. First they man-handled their small boat through choppy seas to reach the rocky islands. It took numerous trips to haul their gear up the slippery, sheer cliffs amidst landing and departing seabirds and their raucous screaming. They had to winch up and secure their dory to the rocks, lest the pounding surf claim it and leave them marooned.

They camped on the island a month, documenting the rich seabird life and their slaughter by weekend gunners on passing party boats that took delight in shooting the nesting birds. Finley observed "The beaches at Oceanside were littered with dead birds following the Sunday carnage." The impassioned Finley took these photos across the nation to an excited President Theodore Roosevelt, who reportedly roared "Bully! Bully!" when he saw the stunning images and declared Three Arch Rocks the first refuge in the West in 1907.

Their photographs of nesting waterfowl at Malheur (Oregon) and Klamath (Oregon and California), and Finley's stories about their devastation by plume hunters, also reached the president's desk and he set aside both as refuges in 1908, the largest established to date.

Finley's advocacy included shrewdly written popular articles and documentary films that included both cute animal stories and serious pieces. He helped establish the Audubon Society of Oregon, the state's first environmental education program. In 1919 he was fired from his post as a state game warden for his outspoken views about the draining of the Klamath Basin. His advocacy succeeded years later at Malheur, where he helped the Bureau to purchase the strategically located P Ranch and its water rights, reviving the historic wetland. This man who experienced thrills climbing 130-foot trees to photograph nesting herons and mingled with the president described the P Ranch purchase as ". . . among my personal highpoints."

△ Atlantic puffin and tern populations on the Maine coast were decimated by aggressive herring and great black-backed gulls. Petit Manan National Wildlife Refuge uses sound recordings and decoys to lure nesting terns and puffins back to islands where gulls are controlled. It works. The two puffins on the right are real; the rest are decoys.

△ After plunging into the ocean from heights of thirty feet or more to catch fish, an arctic tern brings the briny prize to his mate huddled on the nest. To protect the chicks, the parents aggressively discourage intruders, even striking at them to drive them away. Focused restoration efforts are helping to return terns to Maine, located at the southern extent of their breeding range.

△ After spending much of their life at sea, Laysan albatross return to their island namesake to nest. Their colonies are so dense that patches of the island appear to be flocked in white. Though most breed in the remote Hawaiian Islands National Wildlife Refuge, this pair is among a growing number of nesting birds at Kilauea Point (Kauai). Laysan albatross are known to make trips to Aleutian waters to fish. Special salt glands allow them to drink seawater during their ocean journeys. ▷ A Hawaiian monk seal enjoys a respite from the sharks that sometimes surround several of the remote Hawaiian islands. The sharks still take a toll, but the endangered seals are rebounding on several islands where Coast Guard facilities have been removed and disturbance has been eliminated.

Native Hawaiians call the monk seal "Ilioholoikauaua,"

or dog running in the surf. This puppy-faced marine mammal

that rides the waves depends almost entirely on

refuge islands to rest and raise its young.

Monk Seal

Guided by the bright star Arcturus, early Polynesians in long voyaging canoes followed star paths north from Tahiti to the Hawaiian Archipelago, a scattering of subtropical isles formed of sand or by lava spewed by ocean vents spanning a distance of 1,600 miles. Powered by muscle and wind-stroked sails, these ancestors navigated the ocean wilderness by wayfinding, using an ancient culture's memorized knowledge of the wind, sea, sun, and stars to guide them. They arrived at an island paradise of lush rain forests, lava-draped mountains, and palm-studded beaches fringed by coral reefs. Seabirds wheeled in great flocks, sea turtles lumbered across beaches, and monk seals dozed on isolated shores.

Named for the roll of fat arrayed like a monk's cowl around its neck, or as some researchers humorously suggest, the near-monastic life required to study its isolated populations, the monk seal is a living fossil, the most ancient member of the family that includes walrus, seals, and sea lions. The seven-foot long, short-furred seals once flourished in the remote islands and atolls arcing northwest across the Pacific Ocean. Europeans then found them, first sailors shipwrecked on the wind and wave-battered reefs and shores, and then sealing expeditions, feather hunters, fishermen, guano (bird droppings used for fertilizer) harvesters, and others. Monk seals that hauled out to avoid sharks, their biggest threat at sea, found a new menace ashore. Lacking experience with a land predator, the susceptible seals were easily slaughtered and by the early 1900s, few could be found.

Help came in 1909, when President Theodore Roosevelt established the Hawaiian Islands Bird Reservation, eventually renamed the Hawaiian Islands National Wildlife Refuge, to safeguard the seabirds' remote island domain. Monk seals

▽ Green sea turtles have hauled out to nest on Hawaiian beaches for one hundred million years. Although they make occasional appearances in the main Hawaiian islands, these ancient creatures return to lay their gooey eggs largely on just two remote refuge islands within French Frigate Shoals. ▷ A loggerhead turtle makes her way up the beach to nest at Archie Carr National Wildlife Refuge (Florida). This narrow, twenty-mile-long sliver of a refuge protects crucial nesting habitat for one-quarter of the sea turtles that nest in the United States. It was named to honor the renowned Florida turtle researcher and conservationist.

benefitted from this protection and slowly reappeared, resuming their comfortable cycle of surfing to shore, snoozing in the sun, and cooling off in the sea. From December to mid-August pregnant females, each weighing up to seven hundred pounds, hauled out near shallow water and gave birth to a single, glossy black pup with its eyes open, a full coat of fur, and a big appetite. Mother lived off of her ample blubber, nursing her youngster into a fat silver-gray torpedo and good swimmer in just over a month. In this way their numbers increased and by 1958, aerial and beach counts tallied 1,200 monk seals throughout the refuge islands.

For a while the monk seals at French Frigate Shoals continued to increase, but those on other islands declined, hastening their listing as endangered in 1976. With listing came close coordination with the National Marine Fisheries Service, which oversees recovery of the monk seal and manages its deep ocean habitat, while the Fish and Wildlife Service remains responsible for the islands and near shore habitat. During the past quarter century, this interagency team of scientists have researched monk seals, and observed their numbers wax and wane. Recent declines have been attributed to many sources, from human disturbance and entanglement in fishing lines to decreases in the ocean's productivity, global warming, and disease.

Each of the islands has its own dynamics and resulting management needs. Surveys and studies require lengthy travel by air and boat. To avoid inadvertently transporting insects, rats, and plants to islands that are pristine or have been restored, every vessel is carefully inspected and all clothing must be frozen to kill unwanted hitchhikers. Researchers must be hardy, and able to cope with the friendship of birds and the rigors of solitude.

Researchers found that seals on Tern Island began rebounding almost as soon as the Coast Guard closed its station and departed. The refuge is now working with the Coast Guard to remove old transformers and other equipment laden with oil and toxic chemicals. On Laysan, the staff relocated some of the male monk seals to stop an aggressive, hormone-related behavior called mobbing, where overzealous males injure the females and young, sometimes driving them into shark-infested waters. On Kure, managed by the state of Hawaii, the monk seal was

nearly extinct. To begin rebuilding this struggling population, underweight youngsters were held in a shoreline pen where they were fed, became healthy, and were then released. The refuge also captured starving youngsters from French Frigate Shoals and sent them to Oahu for rehabilitation. The seals recovered with care and calories; then were flown to Kure and set free. Several of these rescued seals are now breeding, and refugewide, their numbers have now swelled to 1,400.

Native Hawaiians call the monk seal *Ilioholoikauaua*, or dog running in the surf. This puppy-faced marine mammal that rides the waves depends almost entirely on refuge islands to rest and raise its young, relying upon the Fish and Wildlife Service and its partners to practice the ancient Hawaiian wisdom, *malama*, and care for the land and sea to assure a balance among all forms of life so the monk seal, and others, can always return. ✶

Sea Turtles

No longer buoyed by the sea, a green turtle drags her 350 pounds of protective shell and flesh onto the sand. Descended from ancestors born 150 million years ago, she regards the beach of her birth with scale-ringed eyes that seem as old as time. At twenty-five years, she is both mature and new to motherhood. She chooses a stretch away from the tide but still close to shore, and with powerful flippers, excavates a pit. She lowers herself into it, digging chambers in the moist soil to shelter as many as 130 plum-sized eggs. She carefully buries them and haphazardly casts sand to camouflage the nest, then inches back to the sea. The process takes about two hours and will be repeated up to a half dozen times during summer, an act of survival that assures at least some of her progeny will escape beach-lashing storms, predation, human disturbance, and other hazards of the land.

At Archie Carr National Wildlife Refuge on Florida's highly developed southeast coast, beach guardians patrol as green and loggerhead sea turtles return to nest. The five-hundred-acre refuge was established in 1990, with help from the renowned sea turtle researcher for whom it was named, because of its high concentration of nesting turtles and the pressing threats of development and disturbance. All of the United States' five species of sea turtles are threatened or endangered. About one-fourth of the nation's sea turtles, sometimes more than twenty thousand, nest on nine miles of protected beaches at Archie Carr.

In the last one hundred years, turtle nesting sites used over the millennia have been converted to residences, hotels, and night clubs. Although Archie Carr safeguards vital beach habitat, this protection is not enough. Research and telemetry are providing crucial answers to many questions, such as the cause of a tumor disease afflicting green turtles or why their nesting numbers may be 2,800 one year and just 200 the next. Studies have documented the effects of egg predation by raccoons and other opportunists, which can claim as much as seventy percent of a beach's hatch. They are also tracking how populations rebound when predators are removed.

At Archie Carr and other turtle nesting areas, education has been crucial. The refuge staff and a cadre of volunteers take the public on cautiously guided turtle walks during the two-month nesting season. They explain how garbage can draw unwanted predators and that disturbing the nesting mothers can cause their retreat to water. They show how beach vehicle tracks can block a hatchling's direct route to the ocean, and why balloons, plastic, and other castoffs can become lethal food substitutes. They also patrol to prevent these problems and address them when they arise.

Artificial lighting can also be deadly, a false signal luring turtles seeking the moonlit ocean in the wrong direction. Archie Carr educates residents and local communities about shielding and turning off night lighting during the nesting season, using everything from newsletters and media stories to informational doorknob hangers at local motels. The refuge and its many partners have even worked with towns and counties to pass and enforce night lighting ordinances. Most long-term residents are happy to help protect these lumbering giants. Record numbers of loggerheads have nested, green turtles are increasing, and even leatherbacks have made a tentative reappearance at this Florida refuge.

Green sea turtles also haul out to lay their gooey eggs at beaches on the other side of the nation. Disturbance is no longer a problem at Tern and East islands within the French Frigate Shoals, where 90 percent of Hawaii's green turtles nest. They are protected within the Hawaiian Islands National Wildlife Refuge, where remoteness and human effort are helping them to rebound.

A century and a half ago, green turtles nests here were raided and the adults killed to make turtle soup or provide shells for adornments and souvenirs. Only a small declining population remained. The Coast Guard left East Island in 1952, the price of a nation's protection paid in discarded metal, debris, concrete, and pollutants. When the green turtle was finally declared endangered in 1978, only sixty-nine nests were found on East Island and none

on Tern Island, where the Coast Guard remained until the following year.

The refuge and the National Marine Fisheries Service, responsible for the green turtle recovery program, have made turtle restoration on both islands a priority. On East Island crews arrive by boat to cut up miles of discarded copper wire that entangles wildlife. The wire is collected in pallet tubs and shipped to Honolulu, 550 miles distant, for recycling. During nesting season a solo researcher with enough food for a few days sleeps in a tent by day and walks the entire twelve-acre island at night to identify and examine nesting females, locate their nests, and monitor the hatchlings. The scientist's only contact is by radio with his or her intended replacement, the two trading places throughout the nesting season. Similar nest monitoring occurs at Tern Island, as well as the nightly job of freeing monk seals, seabirds, and disoriented baby green turtles that become trapped behind the island's old, eroding seawall. Such vigilance has

made a difference: recently, more than 1,200 green turtle nest pits were counted on the two islets.

Within their womb of sand, hatchlings sense the temperature drop and humidity increase and know it is evening, just as they know the route to survival lies toward the bright ocean horizon. Barely larger than a half-dollar, they dig together through the heavy sand, finally boiling out of the nest. If they are not disoriented by lights, turned around by a tire track, or eaten by predators, they will feel the ocean's salty embrace. Swimming with frenzied strokes for thirty-six hours and living off the remnants of their yolk sacs, their tiny flippers must carry them miles past schools of predatory fish and other hazards until the ocean currents meet, where they find shelter in vast mats of seaweed. Where some of them go and how they return remains an enigma. That enough survive so many perils and return to their birthing beaches again and again is, perhaps, the greatest mystery of all. ☙

PIPING PLOVER

Once common along the Atlantic Coast, the piping plover is named for its plaintive, bell-like whistle. When standing still, the stocky, sand-colored shorebird blends with the beach, where it feeds and nests. Even this excellent camouflage could not spare piping plovers, which were first slaughtered by plume hunters and, later, nearly decimated by beach development and recreational disturbance. Beach habitat is vital, for this seasoned traveler weighing less than a bar of soap unerringly navigates hundreds of miles to return to the beach of its birth.

At least a dozen national wildlife refuges, from Monomoy (Massachusetts) to Back Bay (Virginia) protect nesting beaches for the threatened plovers, helping their numbers along the coast to increase to a recent high of 1,280 pairs.

△ *After several hours of laying eggs, a loggerhead turtle returns to the ocean's embrace. More than a dozen Gulf and Atlantic refuges protect habitat for several species of imperiled sea turtles.* △ *The piping plover is known for its plaintive, whistling call. At Parker River National Wildlife Refuge (Massachusetts), a worried parent shepherds a tiny chick along the shore, blocking it from the howling wind and teaching it how to freeze at the sound of her whistle.* ▷ *Large enough to harry a pelican with a pouch full of fish, royal terns at Egmont Key National Wildlife Refuge (Florida) nest shoulder to shoulder in small upland dunes protected by sea oats and other wind-blocking vegetation.* ▷▷ *Long-billed dowitchers, western sandpipers, and dunlins rest in the estuary at Grays Harbor National Wildlife Refuge (Washington) before continuing their northbound spring migration, a distance that can span thousands of miles. A million shorebirds descend on the 1,500-acre refuge at the mouth of the Chehalis River in swirling clouds, some staying only briefly. The small refuge accounts for only 2 percent of the tidal habitat but hosts half of the estuary's birds.*

△ Shorebirds navigating to Washington's Willapa National Wildlife Refuge feed on one side of the bay's narrow peninsula when the mudflats are exposed, then move to the other side to loaf until the next low tide. △ △ The largest concentration of horseshoe crabs in the world descend on Delaware Bay beaches to mate and lay their eggs, providing an easy meal for a ruddy turnstone. A single crab nest may hold four thousand eggs. △ ▽ The ruddy turnstone, which gets its name from flipping stones and shoreline debris in search of insects and other edibles, finds a bonanza of crab eggs for the taking at Bombay Hook National Wildlife Refuge (Delaware). Sometimes a million crabs draw a million shorebirds to the bay.

Shorebirds

Oystercatchers the color of midnight, wandering tattlers cloaked in the grays of a cloudy day, long-billed curlews standing two feet tall, and dainty sandpipers smaller than a dollar bill . . . shorebirds differ in size, color, and methods of forage but all make migrations spanning oceans and hemispheres. Flocks of American golden-plovers leave Argentina's pampas, stopping only briefly before reaching their nesting grounds at Arctic National Wildlife Refuge (Alaska). Bar-tailed godwits gather by the tens of thousands each fall at Yukon Delta (Alaska) to pack in calories for perhaps the longest shorebird migration, a nonstop flight of several days to New Zealand.

To make such prolonged journeys, shorebirds rely on marshes strung like pearls along the coast, and scattered across the nation's interior, to provide respite and a banquet of worms, snails, and other edibles to fuel their travels. Weary shorebirds from Tierra del Fuego (South America) gather at Salt Plains (Oklahoma), crowding onto wetlands and resting on the saline crust of an ancient sea. Quivira National Wildlife Refuge and surrounding areas in Kansas may be the most important stopover area for northern shorebirds in North America, perhaps the Western Hemisphere. Pulses of shorebirds darken the sky, descending to marshes fed by miles of canals and water-control structures managed to deliver water when and where it is needed.

For these companions of the wind, timing is everything. Every May, for only a few weeks, the world's largest assemblage of horseshoe crabs seeks Delaware Bay beaches to breed and shelter their pale green eggs. Synchronized by an instinctual timepiece, millions of northbound shorebirds also arrive in the second-largest shorebird migration corridor in the Western Hemisphere. One of their prime stopovers is Bombay Hook, a 1937 waterfowl refuge established

to protect what have now become the only near-pristine tidal marshes on the highly developed bay. Female crabs with males attached to their backs ride evening high tides ashore, where the pair prepare a nest holding up to four thousand eggs. Other crabs and the tide unearth some of the eggs, providing a meal for over a million red knots, semipalmated sandpipers, ruddy turnstones, and other bay shorebirds. Anticipating fluctuations in horseshoe crab numbers, twenty years ago the refuge changed water management on portions of its 1,100 acres of impounded freshwater marshes to offer additional food and resting areas for shorebirds. The nonnative plant, giant reed, would take over these managed ponds were it not for a combination of herbicides and determined refuge vigilance.

Three thousand miles to the west, the Pacific Ocean ebbs and flows within California's largest estuary. San Francisco Bay's tidal flats and wetlands host over a million birds during peak migration, the largest population of wintering shorebirds in the Pacific Flyway. Birds rest, feed, and preen against a backdrop of skyscrapers, freeways, condominiums, and other developments that in the 1960s threatened to take over the entire bay. A groundswell of concerned citizens finally prevailed in 1974 and helped establish the nation's first urban refuge, Don Edwards San Francisco Bay, named for the United States Congressman who authored the refuge legislation. A recent $100 million landmark agreement among federal and state agencies, again urged by citizens, will expand the refuge by 9,500 acres and allow wetland restoration on par with Chesapeake Bay, the Mississippi River, and Florida's Everglades.

Existing salt ponds, levees, and islands support the largest breeding populations of avocets and black-necked stilts on the West Coast. The refuge shelters several imperiled species, including the threatened western snowy plover, a small, pale shorebird reliant upon undisturbed coastal habitat for nesting. It is also a major refueling stop for a half million western sandpipers. A two-year study has charted the travels of sandpipers wearing tiny radio transmitters on their backs, from this urban bay to their northern breeding areas. Weighing less than an ounce, western sandpipers must rest and feed every two to six hundred miles. San Francisco Bay sandpipers are among a million shorebirds that stop briefly at Grays

Harbor National Wildlife Refuge (Washington), devouring lush marine life before continuing north through Canada.

About two weeks after leaving San Francisco Bay, they arrive at Alaska ready to fluff their feathers in display, fly fancy figure-eight flights, and sing the throaty trills of courtship. An international treasure of shorebirds nests on many Alaskan refuges, from Selawik in the north, Yukon Flats and Kanuti in the east, to Togiak and Alaska Peninsula in the south. An estimated 3.3 million breed on Yukon Delta, which protects one of the largest expanses of wetland habitat in the Western Hemisphere. The world's entire population of rare bristle-thighed curlews gather on the refuge prior to migration, and 60 percent breed here. Almost all of the world's black turnstones nest on or near the refuge's coastal meadows. Among the gregarious, jubilant birds of many nations are at least a handful of western sandpipers bearing transmitters from San Francisco Bay, determined travelers whose wing beats and appetites are connecting wetlands separated by thousands of miles, but joined by their purposes. ❧

△ *From sand-colored to blood red, from smooth to armored with spines, sea stars thrive in tidepools, on coral reefs, in grassy beds, and other shore habitats.* △ *When fish rise to the surface in the evening at Edwin B. Forsythe National Wildlife Refuge (New Jersey), black skimmers take to the air. Flying inches above the water, the skimmer opens his bill, letting the long lower mandible slice through the water along the surface. This rough treatment would wear most bills down, but the skimmer's lower mandible grows twice as fast as the upper and is always longer. The skimmer feels for its prey by touch, snapping the bill shut and swallowing without missing a wing beat.*

△ The northern elephant seal is the largest aquatic mammal in the world. This young seal at Oregon Islands National Wildlife Refuge weighed about sixty-five pounds at birth. The males can reach two to three tons when they are mature. △ Profiled by the setting sun, the large hooked proboscis (nose) clearly identifies this as a northern elephant seal bull. Like his male counterparts, his tough hide bears the scars of vicious fighting for the right to breed. Elephant seals breed only at a few Pacific Coast locations. The whaling industry once slaughtered seals for their oil, and they disappeared from places like the Farallon Islands. They returned in 1959 and began breeding in 1972. Several hundred are now born each year on the isolated refuge islands.

Western Mountains & Plains

At a high place known to Native people as the backbone of the world, water shapes the landscape. It is the Great Divide, the Continental Divide, a conceptual line that splits the waters of the continent from Alaska, through the Rocky Mountains, to the tip of South America. The Divide guides the flow of the Rio Grande, Arkansas, and other fledgling streams, sending some east and others west. Divide peaks also shape the region's climate. As ferocious Pacific storms meet the Rocky Mountains, they drop much of their moisture on its forested western flank. Robbed of their load of moisture, the storms continue east, reduced to howling winds that speed across a flat and arid land.

The Divide is more than fifty miles to the west but its influence is keenly felt at Benton Lake National Wildlife Refuge (Montana), where the glacier-scoured terrain includes potholes, a five-thousand-acre marsh, and miles of shortgrass prairie. Sportsmen successfully lobbied twice to protect the drought-prone area, in 1929 to establish

△ *No animal is more intimately tied to the western plains and its Native tribes than the American bison. More than sixty million once roamed the West, providing sustenance for the hungry and warmth against storms and knifing wind. In 1908, the American Bison Society helped establish the National Bison Range (Montana) with funds for land and forty-two bison. Today, more than four hundred flourish where once so few remained.*

a refuge to keep the land in public ownership, and again in 1959, to gain Congressional funds for improvements to bring seasonal water to the migratory birds. To accomplish this, the refuge spends $80,000 annually to pump water from Muddy Creek, fifteen miles to the west, to fill the marsh for the tens of thousands of ducks, geese, swans, and shorebirds that depend upon it for resting, foraging, and often breeding. At times water entering the refuge contains high levels of selenium from fertilizer that can be toxic to wildlife. Periodically, the refuge dries out the wetlands and burns its vegetation to reduce selenium concentrations. They've also worked with farmers, encouraging practices that can reduce the amount of selenium entering the watershed. The wildflower-strewn prairie is occasionally rejuvenated with prescribed burns. Since the 1970s, the refuge has also seeded six hundred acres of croplands in mixed wheat grass and alfalfa to create lush, diverse stands attractive to nesting waterfowl, revitalizing them with periodic haying.

East of Benton Lake, the effect of the Divide rain shadow extends over two hundred miles. Low rainfall produces buffalo grass and other prairie plants that hug the ground to survive cycles of frigid and searing wind. Rainfall gradually increases farther to the east, and with it, the height of the prairie. A sea of tallgrass prairie once covered a quarter of the Lower 48 states. Early explorers were staggered by grass so tall that men on horseback were hidden from view, and so vast it reached the horizon.

The tallgrass prairie was a place of intricate harmony, where life abounded. Elk and bison constantly wandered, sparing the land from overgrazing, each step tilling the soil to foster new growth. Seeds caught in the bison's shaggy coats fell off where they wallowed, germinating with next rainfall. Armies of mice, gophers, and prairie dogs tunneled runways through the grass, and burrows they excavated improved drainage and aerated the soil. Occasional wildfires removed duff and trees, maintaining the prairie's vitality. Beneath the surface, horizontal roots extended for two or three miles. On a hot day it was sometimes twenty degrees cooler underground, the soil insulating the roots from fire and drought. In this dark world insects, grubs, fungi, bacteria, and other organisms aerated and built more

soil. An acre of grassland might support thousands of passing bison while below, in some places, millions of iridescent-veined earthworms and other microorganisms improved tons of soil a year.

As amber fields of grain replaced the native green, this superb balance was destroyed. Of the original 142 million acres of prairie, approximately 10 percent remains untouched by the plow. The tallgrass prairie is even more imperiled. Once covering 85 percent of Iowa, less than 1 percent now endures. Tallgrass prairies in other states are also ailing, making this the most endangered ecosystem in North America.

When it was established in 1991, the charge for Iowa's Neal Smith National Wildlife Refuge was unprecedented in the National Wildlife Refuge System: to discover the processes that sustain the tallgrass prairie ecosystem and reconstruct one, on a landscape scale, in the nation's scarred heartland. This has required the skills of a detective, the training of a botanist, and the talents of a farmer. With only a dozen known prairie remnants in the state's heritage database, the refuge

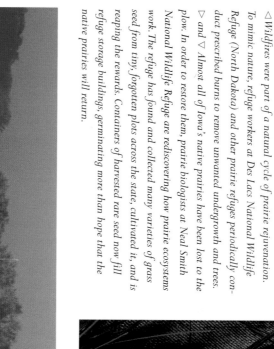

△ Wildfires were part of a natural cycle of prairie rejuvenation. To mimic nature, refuge workers at Des Lacs National Wildlife Refuge (North Dakota) and other prairie refuges periodically conduct prescribed burns to remove unwanted undergrowth and trees.

▽ and ▽ Almost all of Iowa's native prairies have been lost to the plow. In order to restore them, prairie biologists at Neal Smith National Wildlife Refuge are rediscovering how prairie ecosystems work. The refuge has found and collected many varieties of grass seed from tiny, forgotten plots across the state, cultivated it, and is reaping the rewards. Containers of harvested rare seed now fill refuge storage buildings, germinating more than hope that the native prairies will return.

hired and trained five seed seekers, who located more than two thousand new sites in three months. Volunteers from all walks of life have been trained to collect, clean, and label seeds. Small plantings and test plots now form a merging mosaic on 5,300 acres of refuge land. Many aspects of the process are being documented and considered, right down to the fungus required to nurture the roots of the white-fringed prairie orchid and the specific hawkmoth that pollinates this delicate flower. The refuge's Prairie Learning Center is becoming an educational touchstone, allowing farmers' sons and daughters to see how restoring native habitat can enrich their lives, and help their communities. Visitors have watched the tired earth and eroded gullies become recovering prairies and savannahs that nurture the soil, where rare regal fritillary butterflies again light on prairie violets and herds of reintroduced bison and elk wade into tall muhley grass. Workers here, and at Hamden Slough (Minnesota), Northern Tallgrass Prairie (Minnesota), and other prairie refuges, know they must act now or they will never again have the chance to re-create this fragile ecosystem. These are each living laboratories, where refuge workers are tilling minds and healing the land for the bicentennial to come.

Several of the system's oldest refuges were founded in this region with a purpose, hope, and only a tiny reservoir of remaining resource to protect. The National Bison Range (Montana) began with relocated bison, elk, and pronghorn. The National Elk Refuge (Wyoming) was established to save the dwindling Jackson Hole elk. The droughts in the prairie pothole region, North America's principle duck factory, made recovery seem impossible, but refuges such as J. Clark Salyer (North Dakota), Sand Lake (South Dakota), and others led the way. This region of tall mountains, vast plains, and large animals in huge gatherings has bred refuges of great stature, with generations of refuge workers and supporters equal to these challenges. ✔

△ △ *The mountain bluebird visits Crescent Lake National Wildlife Refuge (Nebraska), along with its eastern cousin.* △ ▽ *A cardinal rests on a huisache tree, a common sight at Brazoria and San Bernard National Wildlife Refuges in Texas.* △ ▷ *Its melodic, flutelike song is a signature of the western meadowlark, which nests on the ground and sometimes gathers in large flocks.*

Songbirds

In the 1950s, Coast Guard radar specialists watching Texas and Louisiana shores were occasionally mystified by moving patterns of expanding and contracting shapes that ghosted across their screens. Lacking another explanation, they called them angels. Eventually the shapes were identified as clouds of migrating birds, descending on the Gulf Coast by the millions.

Each spring these featherlight travelers leave their wintering sites in Mexico and Central America and cross the Gulf of Mexico, a perilous five-hundred-mile journey they make without stopping. When fierce head winds force huge flocks to congregate, the weary birds drop out of the sky together at the first coastal landfall, a dramatic appearance called a fallout. Daylight reveals every bush, tree, or vine in a region festooned with exhausted birds clad in ruby, emerald, sapphire, and other gemstone colors. They descend on Aransas, Laguna Atascosa, and mid-Texas coastal refuges by the millions, each sanctuary legendary for its number and diversity of songbirds.

Countless migrants once found shelter in the lichen-bearded grandfather trees of bottomland hardwood forests bordering river floodplains and deltas that once covered a thousand square miles in Texas and Louisiana. Farming, logging, and development have taken their toll; barely one-fourth of this flooded Columbia Bottomland remains, scattered between Atchafalaya National Wildlife Refuge (Louisiana) and the mideast Texas coast. Protecting this imperiled habitat has been a special focus of San Bernard National Wildlife Refuge (Texas), where the refuge, other agencies, and landowners are working to save about seventy thousand acres of bottomlands. More than ten thousand acres have already been protected and are being restored within the refuge. Millions of summer tanagers, Baltimore orioles, and other songbirds now pluck insects and catch a nap on bottomland branches at San Bernard before dispersing throughout the eastern United States.

Protection of another diminishing forest habitat has been vital for one of the nation's most endangered songbirds. The male Kirtland's warbler is known for his repertoire of bubbly, low-pitched calls, sometimes singing as many as two thousand a day. His finicky mate nests only at the base of young jack pines in northern Michigan that are five to twenty feet tall, and about as old in years. A single pair needs eight acres for nesting, and forty acres to raise their young. Periodic wildfires normally killed mature trees and opened the seeds to create patchy, new stands, but by the 1950s, decades of fire suppression left fragmented stands in only eight northern counties.

The resulting decline in Kirtland's warblers was accelerated by aggressive cowbirds, which laid their eggs in the warblers' nests. Generations of dainty warblers hastened their own demise, raising large cowbird youngsters instead of their own. The warblers were declared endangered in 1973 and the following year, only 167 could be counted. Since 1972, the Fish and Wildlife Service has removed almost 125,000 cowbirds and purchased 119 tracts of private inholdings within the state forests. Seney National Wildlife Refuge (Michigan) manages these tracts with the state, each year clear-cutting about two thousand acres of jack pine and replanting trees to mimic the effects of wildfire. The warblers have responded, with about three-fourths nesting in these managed forests. Each spring biologists guided by compasses and maps walk census routes in search of the elusive birds, listening for the singing males to make population estimates. The recovery goal of one thousand pairs was reached in the last two years, a clear sign that the plucky songster is making a guarded comeback.

Fire is also vital to the Baird's sparrow, which leaves Mexico to breed only in a narrow strip of mixed prairie grasses in North Dakota's pothole country. Poor soil and frequent fires spared much of the area from wetland drainage and the plow. More than twenty-six thousand acres were protected at Lostwood National Wildlife Refuge in 1935, where the knobby landscape is large enough for the

breeding dances of sharp-tailed grouse, the courtship displays of shorebirds and waterfowl, and the secret nests of Baird's sparrows. Once the most abundant prairie bird in the area, this elusive sparrow that runs like a mouse to hide from predators has lost much of its essential prairie. Snowberries and other nonnative trees have slowly colonized parts of the formerly treeless prairie, providing an environment for invasive grasses to proliferate. The refuge conducts the largest prescribed fire program in the region to help this rare sparrow and other prairie birds, using fire to tame the woodlands, fight alien species, and reinvigorate the prairie grasses.

Hundreds of refuges have been established to aid migratory birds. As the concept of preserving biodiversity has taken hold, a growing number of refuges have focused on songbird conservation. Balcones Canyonlands (Texas) was established to save the nesting habitat of the endangered golden-cheeked warbler and black-capped vireo. Research

programs at Montezuma and Iroquois (New York) are looking at the special needs of cerulean warblers. Surveys and habitat protection are helping Henslow's sparrows at Big Oaks (Indiana). Management of wetlands and forests at Santa Ana (Texas) are preserving unique subtropical habitat laden with species found few other places on earth.

Songbirds are deeply embedded in the human experience. Their music is the symphony of a sunrise, the throbbing richness of a spring day, the voice of the forest. For a century, national wildlife refuges have given them sanctuary, preserving the tradition of their courageous flights, and the cherished legacy of their songs. ☙

▽ *North America's most abundant warbler, the yellow-rumped warbler is common at refuges in the west, south, and northeastern regions of the country. The gregarious birds travel and feed in large winter flocks that look like yellow streaks moving through the forest canopy.*

ATTWATER PRAIRIE CHICKEN

Their dance was copied by the Plains Indians. Their booming calls announced spring on the Texas and Louisiana prairie. A century ago, up to a million Attwater prairie chickens gathered at their traditional prairie breeding grounds. The males held their tails erect, and puffed out air sacs on their necks, making a booming sound. They shuffled, stomped, and fought with other males, an annual rite to win a mate.

Once free to roam over six million acres, their numbers waned as the prairies were lost to farming, development, and industry. They disappeared from Louisiana in 1919 and only 8,700 could be counted in 1937. Shortly after their 1967 endangered species listing, the World Wildlife Fund purchased 3,500 acres and transferred it to the U.S. Fish and Wildlife Service to create the Attwater Prairie Chicken National Wildlife Refuge (Texas).

Despite these measures, in 1992 researchers found only 456 wild birds, and a captive breeding program was initiated. Just 42 remained in 1996, when the first captive-reared chicks were released. Their numbers have now edged up to 58. The refuge annually burns up to three thousand acres and collects native grass seed to help rejuvenate the prairie. They control predators and, much like natural prairie ecosystems, use bison and cattle to groom the prairie and create openings used as travel routes by the tiny chicks.

△ A male Attwater prairie chicken holds his tail erect and uses air sacs to boom his intentions as he performs an energetic dance to attract a mate. The prairie chicken was declared endangered because less than 1 percent of the coastal prairie habitat it requires now remains. The Attwater Prairie Chicken National Wildlife Refuge (Texas) protects more than seven thousand acres, a highly managed sanctuary for wild and captive-bred and released birds.

▷ A monarch butterfly feeds on goldenrod along the Atlantic shore. Thousands may rest on a single tree. Their closed wings are a somber gray, but as the morning sun warms them, the tree pulses with the brilliant orange of fluttering wings. These featherlight beauties are found across North America. Their migrations are legendary, some of the tiny travelers covering four thousand miles during a round-trip migration.

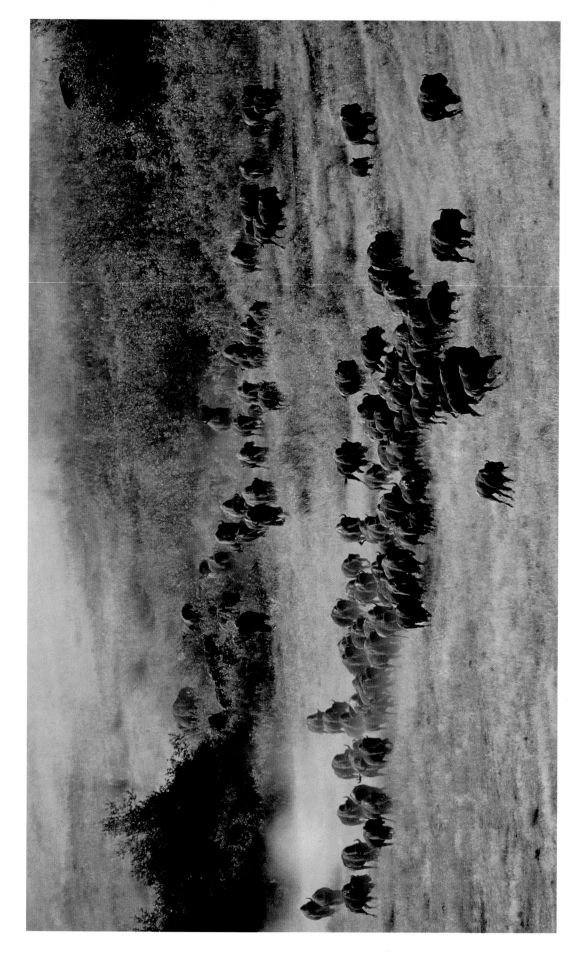

△ *Bison now thrive at National Bison Range (Montana) and Wichita Mountains (Oklahoma), Fort Niobrara (Nebraska), and Sullys Hill (North Dakota) National Wildlife Refuges, each established to protect the woolly mammals nearly a century ago. Populations are kept in check with periodic roundups. Mounted riders and sometimes helicopters gather the herd, then drive it to an enclosure where animals are medically sampled and sorted for auction or release on the refuge. △ Protected by a thick coat from searing heat and chilling wind, a bison cow and her calf browse on prairie grasses that have likewise evolved to withstand temperature extremes. A newborn weighing twenty to seventy pounds can weigh over five hundred pounds at one year.*

At one time the American bison roamed the prairies and grasslands

in staggering numbers of sixty million or more. This ton of muscle

covered with tough hide was uniquely adapted to the prairie,

its feet stirring seeds in the soil and its drive to wander

protecting the landscape from overgrazing.

American Bison

On October 18, 1907, a New York train bearing precious cargo labored to a stop in the small southwestern Oklahoma town of Cache. Led by the renowned Comanche Chief Quanah Parker, Indians on horseback joined excited throngs of townspeople gathered to witness this historical moment. Heavy crates bearing fifteen healthy bison donated from the New York Zoological Park were placed on mule-drawn wagons for the thirteen-mile trip to a fenced enclosure in the Wichita Forest. It had been fifty years since the last bison were slaughtered on these wild prairies. An icon of the Great Plains had returned.

At one time the American bison roamed the prairies and grasslands in staggering numbers of sixty million or more. This ton of muscle covered with tough hide was uniquely adapted to the prairie, its feet stirring seeds in the soil and its drive to wander protecting the landscape from overgrazing. Bison were the heart of the Plains Indian's existence and spiritual life. Their dried droppings fueled fires, woolly hides became robes and moccasins, meat and marrow were a source of sustenance.

Between 1840 and 1890, bison numbers plummeted. Traders bartered with the Indians, sometimes securing a hide for as little as three cups of coffee or six cups of sugar. Hide hunters followed, often taking fifty to a hundred animals a day. Then General Phillip Sheridan ordered the Plains Indians into established reservations, making way for the railroad and settlement. Numerous efforts to pass state and federal legislation to protect America's largest game animal failed. After supporting their decimation, in 1894 Congress finally appropriated $15,000 to buy twenty-one privately owned bison to augment Yellowstone National Park's small wild herd. The land was strewn with their bones and less than one hundred wild bison remained.

Recognizing the bison's fragile existence, William Temple Hornaday of the Smithsonian Institution organized the American Bison Society in 1905, with President Theodore Roosevelt as the group's honorary leader. This group and the New York Zoological Society offered to donate fifteen bison if Congress would provide $15,000 to fence an area in Oklahoma's Wichita National Forest and Game Preserve. The fence was built and fifteen wagons unloaded the crated animals, which ambled into freedom and a new future for the American bison.

It is fortunate for the bison, and the relocated elk, longhorn cattle, turkeys, prairie dogs, river otters, and burrowing owls that have followed, that the refuge's oak savannah and prairie had been too rocky to till and were set aside as a sanctuary. In the early years, the refuge and Civilian Conservation Corps crews expanded the fencing to encompass the entire fifty-nine-thousand-acre refuge, constructed working pens, and built stock ponds, water impoundments, and concrete dams to hold year-round water. The refuge provided supplemental feeding for about two decades, until the native prairie was healthy. This careful husbandry continues today, and now six hundred bison roam the Wichita refuge.

The refuge has since separated the herd into three groups with cross fencing. Each October the stillness of the prairie is broken by a distant drumming. The sound of hooves beating the earth draws closer, accompanied by a smear of dust on the horizon. The air vibrates with bellowing as hundreds of the shaggy beasts appear, trotting ahead of a hovering helicopter and cowboys mounted on sturdy horses. The standard story is that a cowboy can drive the bison anywhere they want to go. The route is never direct; bison constantly veer to the left and the right to keep sight of their pursuers.

The refuge culls out older animals to auction, samples for diseases, and shuffles youngsters between the herds to maintain genetic diversity. Since 1907, more than seven thousand excess animals have been sold or donated to preserve the high quality of Wichita grasslands.

A year after the bison came to Wichita, the American Bison Society urged the President to establish the National Bison Range in Montana. The Society raised $10,000 to purchase a private herd of forty-two animals that were moved to the refuge. The herd has swelled to 450, a number maintained by periodic roundups. Animals are tested, sampled, and tiny tags are inserted beneath the skin to identify each animal. All of the bison on refuges and other public lands are descended from the same early herds. While some mixing with cattle has occurred with private herds, those on public lands remain pure, a genetic legacy descended from the same stock that once roamed the Old West.

The American Bison Society disbanded in 1918, having met their goal of saving the bison. There are now about 25,000 on public lands and over 180,000 on private ranches in the United States and Canada. Several other refuges are also bison guardians, including Sully's Hill (North Dakota), Fort Niobrara (Nebraska), and Neal Smith (Iowa). At these refuges, people are learning about the intimate relationship between the bison and rare prairie ecosystems. It is a symbiotic joining that the Plains Indians have understood since the beginning of their time. For them, the spirit of the bison, the Indian, and the earth are one. Private herds may wax and wane, but several national wildlife refuges and other sanctuaries will assure that this soul of the earth endures. ✦

▽ Like other male deer and elk, mule deer bucks carry a set of branched antlers that can become massive. Bucks shed their antlers during winter, after the "rut," when bucks spar for the right to breed. New antlers begin forming in spring, and are made of bone covered with a furlike skin that nourishes them. When the antler stops growing, the velvet dies and often hangs in tatters until the buck rubs it off on trees and brush.
▷ Faded coloring helps protect shorebirds from predation. The American avocet is an exception, wearing bright cinnamon, black, and white from spring until summer's end. Shorebirds are not just associated with the coast. Huge concentrations rely on the country's interior wetlands, from Yukon Flats National Wildlife Refuge (Alaska) and Quivira (Kansas) to Stillwater in Nevada's high desert.

△ Balancing on stiltlike legs, greater sandhill cranes at Bosque del Apache National Wildlife Refuge (New Mexico) feed on marshes created with water pumped from the Rio Grande. Refuge workers vigilantly remove tamarisk and other invasive species. They also plant grains and corn to supplement the natural fare. Protection and management have helped cranes increase from as few as 17 in 1941 to more than 13,000 today, a spectacle celebrated at an annual refuge festival.

Sandhill Crane

Faint, tremulous calls float from above the clouds, an ancient song bugled by red-capped nomads traveling skies that link their seasonal homes. The extra long windpipe of these high sky callers allows the sandhill crane's haunting music to carry, resonating across miles. As the weather warms in North America, a half-million gregarious sandhill cranes gather on the grasslands, cultivated fields, and braided channels of Nebraska's Platte River to rest and build their fat reserves for the spring migration. When the time nears to depart for Canada, Alaska, and Siberia, excited birds trumpet and bounce, then spiral thousands of feet on thermals to exercise their wings, before rejoining the flock.

A similar, but smaller, spectacle is staged at Bosque del Apache National Wildlife Refuge (New Mexico). About thirteen thousand wintering cranes have drawn thousands of visitors and been celebrated at an annual festival embraced by the community. In the spring they depart for Alamosa/Monte Vista (Colorado), joining others to roost in the refuges' managed marshes and feed on grains planted to fuel their flights north.

With graceful necks outstretched and legs fully extended, a contingent of these primordial-looking birds then ride the wind to a remote Idaho valley edged by high, forested peaks and shrub-dotted slopes. Ice may still mantle the grasses and shallows of Gray's Lake, but courting pairs of sandhill cranes are undeterred as they bow, leap, toss nesting materials, and sing their guttural duets. Grays Lake, the largest hardstem bulrush marsh in North America, is also home to the highest density of nesting greater sandhill cranes in the world. As many as 250 pairs trust the barrier of water and wide open vistas to provide roosting and nesting areas that are safe from predators. While places such as the Yukon Delta (Alaska) may see ten thousand nesting cranes, spread over millions of acres, those at Grays Lake jam into a fraction of the space.

Grays Lake National Wildlife Refuge was established in 1965 to safeguard the cranes and legions of other waterbirds. Almost a century of water diversions have periodically threatened this wetland. For decades the refuge has worked closely with the Bureau of Indian Affairs, which controls the water drawdowns, to balance the seasonal needs of wildlife with demands for water from surrounding communities. Lacking the prolific muskrat populations that once inhabited the marsh and excavated openings, the refuge staff helps nature along by developing open areas, ponds, and islands to maintain the area's appeal to cranes and other waterbirds. They allow haying and livestock grazing, conduct prescribed burns to groom the grasslands, and sweeten the refuge's attraction with planted barley and other grains that encourage the birds to remain.

Many other refuges are important to sandhill cranes. More than one hundred thousand may winter at Muleshoe (Texas). Nearly half of the world's population, some two hundred thousand birds, stop over at Tetlin (Alaska). They gather by the thousands in the west at Columbia (Washington) and San Luis (California). Success is also measured in smaller numbers. At urban Stone Lakes (California), located a dozen miles from downtown Sacramento, grazing and wetland restoration programs are revitalizing habitat and 150 foraging and roosting cranes have returned after more than a decade of absence. In Mississippi, intense management is helping to reestablish a race of sandhill cranes found nowhere else in the wild.

This genetically distinct strain of sandhill cranes once found along coastal areas of central Gulf states diminished to only six nesting pairs as the wet pine savannahs that sustained them were converted to pine plantations or housing subdivisions. Their almost certain extinction was publicized by Jake Valentine, a seasoned Fish and Wildlife Service employee who understood the birds' dependency on what had become one of the rarest ecosystems in North America.

Beginning in 1965, a captive flock was established at the Patuxent Wildlife Research Center using one egg taken from selected wild nests, leaving the second egg for the nesting pair to raise. The cranes were declared endangered in 1973, and two years later, the Mississippi Sandhill Crane Refuge was established to protect a legacy of no more than thirty-five wild birds. The first captive-reared birds were released on the refuge in 1981, in what has become the largest and most enduring crane reintroduction program in the world. The refuge staff have used hand tools and prescribed burns to remove thousands of acres of slash pines to revitalize the rare wet pine savannah. They have created new roosting ponds and planted supplemental food for the growing flock. Seasonal predator control is giving vulnerable chicks and newly released birds a better chance. Today, re-created wet pine savannahs abounding with orchids and other native plants sustain 120 cranes, including twenty-five nesting pairs, the beginnings of a guarded comeback.

For eons, the spirit of the elegant sandhill crane has been captured on canvas, in sculpture, and through dance, Yoga, and the martial arts. For a hundred years, national wildlife refuges have helped to assure that its living counterpart survives, thrives, and flies free. ☞

△ As the sun sets, sandhill cranes congregate to roost in a shallow wetland or field where they can see approaching predators.

△ Their route illuminated by a full moon, migrating sandhill cranes glide on thermal currents between their breeding and winter homes. They mark their progress with steady wing beats and a chorus of distant, rattling calls.

Jake Valentine

Everything about Jake Valentine was big: his size, his talent, his passion, and the types of biological challenges that he tackled. He spent much of his career working at the southeast refuges, eventually becoming the Gulf Coast regional biologist. During his tenure, he followed and chronicled the advance of oil fields and the development of the Intracoastal Waterway and other barge canals.

He learned about each of the region's Native peoples and knew the local heroes. He was as comfortable talking with muskrat farmers as he was with state legislators. He watched cycles of droughts, changing seasons heralded by waterfowl, and the advance of refuges he knew well, such as Lacassine (Louisiana), Delta (Louisiana), and the Arthur R. Marshall Loxahatchee National Wildlife Refuge in the Florida Everglades.

The wet pine savannah habitat of Mississippi was diminishing, unique habitat required by an endangered race of sandhill cranes found only in this region of Mississippi. Some unaltered savannah remained in Jackson County, the breeding grounds for a small flock of nonmigratory cranes.

Valentine was asked to investigate the potential effects of constructing Interstate 10 on this remnant crane population. He documented the severe habitat decline, described the risk to the cranes, and called for creation of a refuge for them. The "cranes versus lanes" controversy during the 1970s was an uphill battle at times, involving cessation of the interstate construction while a federal court case was heard. Those who know him claim that without Valentine's expertise, courage, and single-minded determination, there would be no Mississippi Sandhill Crane National Wildlife Refuge.

Valentine maintained an interest in the cranes the rest of his career, retaining his reputation as a legend well into his mid-seventies.

▷ *The American kestrel is North America's smallest falcon.*

△ *Winter wagon or sleigh rides capture the thrill of bygone years at the National Elk Refuge (Wyoming), where visitors enjoy a horse-drawn ride into Rocky Mountain elk country. The refuge shelters nearly 7,500 elk, the largest gathering of its kind in the world. The staff makes the natural grasslands as productive as possible through seeding, prescribed burning, and irrigation. When deep snow covers the grasslands, they feed the elk palletized alfalfa for several months, often up to thirty tons each day.*

△ and ▷ △ ▷ Foothills rise into the forest-clad mountains and granite peaks of the Teton Range, a dramatic backdrop for trumpeter swans at the National Elk Refuge (Wyoming). The huge birds made a comeback at Red Rock Lakes (Montana) and through relocation have expanded their range. Trumpeter swans nest and winter at the National Elk Refuge.

For all of their size and command of the skies,

trumpeter swans can be extremely wary

and shun areas that are disturbed.

Trumpeter Swan

I n 1876 near Yellowstone National Park, pioneers homesteaded a secluded valley dappled with lakes and ringed by rugged mountains and sage-covered horizons. In honor of their nation's birthday, they named the valley Centennial. The region's forests and plains were rich with moose, elk, and pronghorn, and its wetlands were thick with waterfowl. Even from a distance of two miles, homesteaders could see flocks of great white birds rising from the water, carried aloft by wings spanning eight feet, and hear the birds' deep, melodious calls. These were trumpeter swans, the largest waterfowl in the world. This valley became one of their last strongholds, and the location of a comeback achieved during another centennial, the first one hundred years of the National Wildlife Refuge System.

For all of their size and command of the skies, trumpeter swans can be extremely wary and shun areas that are disturbed. The Centennial Valley provided the seclusion they required to breed and raise their fuzzy gray cygnets. The snowmelt-fed lakes yielded a feast of aquatic creatures and plants. When fierce winter storms froze the landscape, the swans congregated on ponds and streams heated by warm springs with enough greens and cover to see the swans through the harshest winters. Such abundance made migration unnecessary and many swans stayed year-round. Those that migrated were shot, or lost wintering habitat to settlement, and the tradition of migration was lost.

Like other feathered cousins, the trumpeter swan was stalked for its plumage, meat, skin, and eggs. By 1912, the stunning ivory bird, with an extra loop in its windpipe responsible for its deep call, was considered extinct. Seven years later, a Yellowstone National Park employee shocked the world by sighting of a pair with three cygnets in a back-country wilderness people had not yet discovered.

The first aerial survey of the Yellowstone region in 1932 produced a count of just sixty-nine birds, with about half in the Centennial Valley. In 1935 President Franklin D. Roosevelt established Red Rock Lakes National Wildlife Refuge in the heart of the valley to help the ailing swans. Much of the refuge is a Wilderness Area, offering added protection from disturbance. Early refuge staff controlled grazing to yield the short-grass habitat swans prefer, curtailed poaching, and revived muskrat populations so the swans could once again build nests atop their lodges.

Uncertain that this tiny legacy of swans could survive the winter, in the 1930s the refuge began a feeding program that endured until 1992. Twice a week all season, refuge workers in boats scattered bushels of wheat or barley on the two unfrozen ponds, drawing hundreds of birds. Soon swan numbers began to increase by about 10 percent a year, eventually expanding to populate a small tristate region (Montana, Idaho, and Wyoming). Refuge birds were joined each winter by other tristate birds, all drawn to the grains and warm pond habitat.

The supplemental feeding allowed the sanctuary to support many more swans than nature had intended. To reduce stress on the habitat and establish flocks elsewhere, more than 1,300 swans have been captured at Red Rock Lakes and nearby Harriman State Park, and relocated to Lacreek (South Dakota), Seney (Michigan), and other refuges and natural areas, where they are now reproducing.

Red Rock Lakes no longer feeds the swans, hoping to break this dependency and encourage other tristate birds to migrate. While recently declining swan numbers on the refuge are a concern, in the space of seven decades, trumpeter swan numbers have increased to 3,000 in the Lower 48 states. A surprise 1954 discovery of 1,100 breeding swans in Alaska has grown to 14,000, another safety net for the once-imperiled birds.

The Red Rock Lakes swans remain unique, the only indigenous flock in the Lower 48 and a living relic of a nation's rich past. Each fall another generation of youngsters points their heads into the wind and urgently flaps unseasoned wings as they race across the water. The miracle of lift occurs and initial awkwardness is transformed into a flight of easy grace. Young and old birds trumpet their pleasure with low, rich calls, at a national wildlife refuge that has assured their glad voices will be heard. 🐾

▽ *Its wingspan can be as wide as the tallest basketball player, making the trumpeter swan the largest swan in the world. Its size and white coloring also made the trumpeter swan highly vulnerable to feather and hide hunters and egg collectors, who nearly decimated the swans in the Lower 48 states. Red Rock Lakes National Wildlife Refuge (Montana) was established in 1935 largely for the swans. Supplemental feeding and relocations have helped increase their numbers from a low of sixty-nine birds in 1932 to more than three thousand at Red Rock Lakes, other refuges, and natural areas in the Lower 48. This refuge is also known for its diversity, from dainty savannah sparrows and secretive American martens to conspicuous Shiraz moose.*

△ There is nothing surprising about an American badger carrying a ground squirrel, except being in the right place to see one. This mother returned to her burrow where she shared her prize with four hungry youngsters. Most badgers avoid confrontations, but will ferociously defend themselves if they are threatened.

△ An endangered black-footed ferret lives in a natural pen setting at Bowdoin National Wildlife Refuge's (Montana) captive breeding facility. The Charles M. Russell National Wildlife Refuge (Montana) was chosen as a prime black-footed ferret release site because of its nearly one hundred prairie dog towns. Prairie dogs are the primary food source for ferrets, making the black-tailed prairie dog and the black-footed ferret mortal enemies.
▽ After searching for greens or insects, a parent prairie dog greets its pup outside the burrow. They are very social animals, with several thousand living in a single town laced with underground burrows.
▷ The vocal prairie dog has nine different calls, from barks to chirps. This talker has thrown back his head, raised his forelegs, and given a whistling yip, an "all clear" signal that is echoed throughout the town.

BLACK-FOOTED FERRET

Prairie dog towns and black-footed ferrets were once a hallmark of the prairie ecosystem. Ferrets preyed on prairie dogs, relying upon them for sustenance and inhabiting their burrows. As land was converted for agriculture, prairie dogs were shot and poisoned. Sylvatic plague and other threats further reduced their numbers, and ferret populations similarly plummeted.

Nearly extinct, the ferret was declared endangered in 1967. A small population was discovered in 1981, and 18 animals were eventually moved to a captive breeding facility. They were reintroduced at Charles M. Russell National Wildlife Refuge (Montana) in 1994, and six years later, 168 kits had been born in the wild. Unexpectedly, survival and repro-duction crashed, and by spring 2003, only 3 animals remained. Similar losses have occurred with other populations. There are no clear answers but research suggests that sylvatic plague and shortage of large expanses of land with prairie dogs are prime suspects.

Patuxent Wildlife Research Center

Bald eagles, whooping cranes, and Aleutian Canada geese are among more than a dozen imperiled species that have been or are being restored to refuges and other wild places through captive breeding efforts. These complicated programs require highly specialized facilities and trained staff who can devote their time to research, field investigations, and propagation programs.

For many decades Patuxent Wildlife Research Center in Maryland was the largest and perhaps most renowned wildlife research facility in the world. For most of its sixty plus years of existence it was part of the Fish and Wildlife Service. The U.S. Geological Survey has administered the Center since 1996.

Beginning in 1965, Ray Erickson was in charge of the Endangered Species Research Section, a small cadre of scientists who traveled the country studying sixty different species at risk, from Everglades kites (Florida) and black-footed ferrets (South Dakota) to California condors and twenty imperiled species in Hawaii. The Patuxent researchers identified DDT accumulation in bald eagle eggs, then developed methods for incubating the eagles' shatter-prone shells. They removed eggs from early nestings in the wild, allowing the mates to breed again. The borrowed eggs were incubated, and the Patuxent staff nurtured the fragile chicks through their first crucial weeks of life. The center successfully fostered more than 120 chicks with captive-reared bald eagles on elevated platforms, called hacking towers, at natural areas throughout the east.

"We were extremely cautious when working with species whose numbers were so few," recalls Erickson. "Before initiating our work with whooping cranes, we used three races of sandhill cranes to develop safe rearing methods for the whoopers. When we began looking at black-footed ferrets, I made a trip to Russia to pick up four dozen polecats, a similar species, for our initial propagation studies. Whether it's the bald eagle or Aleutian Canada goose, Patuxent has been a sort of Noah's Ark, helping to carry endangered species through periods of adversity and extreme decline in the wild."

The Northern Prairie Wildlife Research Center (North Dakota), also operated by the Fish and Wildlife Service until 1993, has conducted similar research on a wide range of species for almost sixty years.

Southern Shores & Swamps

S horeline is a dynamic boundary, shifting daily as angled waves grab sand from one beach and transport it to another. Deposited off shore, the sand forms a phalanx of barrier islands that stretches from Maine to Texas. Some remain spartan beaches, their coarse sands and low-lying shrubs a gathering and breeding site for water-associated birds. Others collect marine debris and seeds from the surf and passing birds, gradually forming an elevated platform that supports trees, shrubs, and grasses and sustains incredible diversity. Fiddler crabs scuttle among the exposed roots, green turtles eat the fallen leaves, brown pelicans and herons nest in the canopy, diminutive Key deer find shelter among the tangled undergrowth, and weary songbirds traveling from other nations make this their first landfall.

Along the nation's shores, the designing hand of nature also destroys. For decades gulf winds and surf turned belligerent by storms have partially consumed Dressing Point at Big Boggy National Wildlife Refuge (Texas). Here showy roseate spoonbills mix with brown pelicans and sixteen other species of colonial birds. The twelve-acre

△ *Each spring, mangroves on Mullet Head Island become a multistoried brown pelican rookery at Merritt Island National Wildlife Refuge (Florida). Few refuges or other natural areas can match the diversity of bird life at this Atlantic Coast refuge.*

island hosts up to twelve thousand pairs of white ibis, the largest nesting colony in Texas, each pair staking out a nest on the low shrubs or sandy beach. To rebuild and protect this vital rookery, refuge staff and volunteers have hauled cement riprap by boat, positioned it to halt erosion, and planted smooth cordgrass to protect the island's southwest shore.

The same storms that nibble at islands replenish streams and rivers that flow into the coastal estuaries. The rain also floods inland wetlands underlain by limestone, peat, or other water-holding surfaces, forming a spongy swamp populated by water-loving grasses, trees, and shrubs. Swamp air is warm and damp, often supporting orchids, air plants, and other tropical plants. Vegetation clogs waterways that end at cloistered pools. Impenetrable thickets of trees stand in the water, supported by intertwined branches and masses of broad, exposed roots.

Swamps are laced with the pungent scent of decay, the slow pulse of decomposition fueling a unique web of life and ancient relationships. The alligator watches as a nesting great blue heron in an old cypress leaves its eggs to find food. A waiting raccoon stalks toward the tree, and the heron's vacated nest. The alligator grabs the unwary raccoon, leaving its gator hole unattended long enough for the heron to spear a fish. Southern swamps nurture life, from legions of insects that mine the tree bark and butterflies sipping nectar to black bears ghosting between trees. Alligators bellow and grunt, frogs sing in choruses, birds trill in harmony. The primordial hum of swamp music is everywhere, softening its reputation as a dark and unfriendly place.

Vast prairies of twelve-foot high sawgrass, winding waterways, and dense tree-covered islands covered by a thin sheet of water define the Everglades, the liquid heart of Florida. The sharp-edged grass is so impenetrable it can only be flattened by a hurricane or excavated by the powerful jaws and snout of nature's engineer, the alligator, whose earthmoving opens channels that aid other swamp travelers.

The cypress and tupelo swamps at Alligator River National Wildlife Refuge (North Carolina) once sustained so many alligators that a river bears their name. Today the refuge marks the northern extent of the American alligator's range, and more recently, the first recovery site

△ Dense cypress-tupelo swamps and the largest remaining bottomland forest in the United States are home to scores of species at Atchafalaya National Wildlife Refuge (Louisiana). A barred owl watches from a flooded cypress forest, where ancient cypress stand on flared bases several times wider than the tops of the trunks. Crevices in these knobby "cypress knees" trap bits of soil, gradually building a base of land to support the trees. ▽ Unaware of the human eyes just a few feet away, a bobcat ghosts onto a secluded path at Santa Ana National Wildlife Refuge (Texas), on the northern edge of the Rio Grande. The small, spotted cat with erect ears is not often seen, making a surprise appearance on a trail winding through the moss-veiled forest.

for the endangered red wolf. With help from concerned citizens and groups, the refuge was established with a 118,000-acre donation by Prudential Life Insurance, following a failed effort to extract peat and drain the swamps and wetlands. It was there just in time to aid the cinnamon-colored wolves, which once ranged throughout the Southeast. The red wolf was declared extinct in 1980, after the Fish and Wildlife Service captured the few remaining in the wild to breed at zoos and begin a recovery program. In 1987, Alligator River's willing refuge staff provided a first home for four pairs. Refuge births, additional reintroductions, and fostering of captive-bred pups have seen their number swell to one hundred animals. The refuge is restoring swamps, and the cedar and bottomland hardwood forests the wolves require. They also trap and sterilize coyotes, which can mate with wolves and produce unwanted genetic hybrids.

With this careful husbandry, the world's free-ranging red wolf population has now expanded to a five-county area, and hope abides for an animal declared extinct just a few decades ago.

A quarter of a million years ago, the Atlantic Ocean extended inland seventy-five miles and then receded, scooping out a vast, shallow depression and depositing sand along ridges in retreat. Over time rains filled the clay-lined basin and generations of plants took hold and died, yielding layers of peat. Located in what is now Georgia and northern Florida, the Seminole Indians called the resulting swamp Okefenokee, the land of trembling earth. Stories about lost gator hunters, dark nights spiked by unearthly grunts and growls, and lore about an island Eden inhabited by beautiful women have spiced stories about this world-famous swamp. Over time it has been ditched, drained, and logged. A 396,000-acre mosaic of unusual landscapes is protected at Okefenokee National Wildlife Refuge. Belts of moss-veiled cypress and peat bogs are connected by dim waterways accented by water lilies, spatter-dock, and swamp irises. Expanses of tea-colored water are broken by odd-shaped islands and hemmed in by yellow-eyed grass, sedges, and pitcher plants. Lightning fires, always extinguished until recently, are closely monitored and now help rejuvenate the swamp by setting back succession and creating open vistas. The refuge staff also conducts prescribed burns to reduce flammable vegetation in critical areas and thin the upland landscape to favor growth of native longleaf pines and a naturally functioning three-hundred-year-old forest. Its wading bird and alligator populations are legendary, and so is the diverse list of imperiled species it sustains, including red-cockaded woodpeckers and indigo snakes.

From parula warblers to hot pink flamingoes, from shy manatees to elusive Florida panthers, southern shores and swamps are rich ecosystems that sustain a sweeping range of wildlife diversity. Some of the world's first sanctuaries, the earliest national wildlife refuges, were born of the need to protect this bounty. Those refuges and many more today, especially dozens in Florida, continue to shield these fragile landscapes from human efforts to tame them, fighting to preserve a heritage of wildness that is often just a stone's throw from a gas station or fast food restaurant. ⌇

National Audubon Society

Many of the earliest refuges, like Pelican Island, were established at the urging of the early Audubon Society and were patrolled by Audubon volunteers and wardens. At least three Audubon wardens lost their lives to bird poachers while defending nesting birds.

The centennial of the National Wildlife Refuge System is also the one hundredth year of partnership between these two organizations. The Audubon Society was formed in 1886 by *Forest and Stream* editor George Bird Grinnell, who named the nation's first bird preservation organization after American naturalist and painter John James Audubon. Other similar societies formed a loose coalition and incorporated in 1905, a modest alliance that has evolved into today's National Audubon Society.

The National Audubon Society and its members have since helped to establish scores of refuges. Audubon has actively promoted laws that guide many refuge purposes, from the Federal Migratory Bird Treaty Act to laws involving clean air, clean water, and endangered species. Refuges and local Audubon chapters cooperate on research projects, community projects, and annual bird counts.

Audubon's members also continue to roll up their sleeves to work. Seventy-five groups participate in a national campaign called Audubon Refuge Keepers that assist refuges in myriad ways. The San Diego chapter helped establish a new management unit within San Diego National Wildlife Refuge. The Salem group is planting trees at Baskett Slough and Ankeny, two Oregon refuges. The Shoals chapter worked with the Girl Scouts to build a new trail at Key Cave (Alabama). And at John Heinz (Pennsylvania) the Wyncote chapter writes fund-raising appeals, having already raised enough to build an environmental center at this urban refuge.

Brown Pelicans

The slender German boatbuilder put down his hammer as soon as he heard shooting near his boat works and home where the Indian River meets the South Florida coast. Armed with a double-barreled shotgun and the strength of his convictions, Paul Kroegel raced in a sailboat or rowboat to stop the sport shooters, plume hunters, commercial fisherman, or egg thieves from further decimating a struggling colony of nesting brown pelicans on a nearby five-acre island. Anytime an influential naturalist visited the nearby Oak Lodge, the mailboat would bring word to Kroegel and he would again drop his hammer to speak with the visitor about getting protection for the beleaguered brown pelicans.

Kroegel, an Audubon Society warden hired to protect birds on Pelican Island, wasn't their only defender. President Theodore Roosevelt heard about Kroegel and Pelican Island from ornithologists and others, and on March 14, 1903, declared Pelican Island the nation's first bird reservation. Two weeks later, Warden Kroegel became the nation's first refuge employee, earning one dollar a month. By the time he died in 1948, this speck of mangroves was again a mecca for nesting birds.

In the 1960s a proposal to fill nearby wetlands was defeated by the refuge and a growing list of allies. By then, pelican numbers were again plummeting because their eggshells became too thin to withstand the weight of the incubating parents. Once common on all three coasts, the only viable North American brown pelican populations were in Florida in 1970,

△△ *An endangered brown pelican shields her young.*
△ *With bills clashing, two brown pelicans settle a nesting dispute.*
△ *Pelican Island National Wildlife Refuge (Florida), a tiny speck of mangroves, was the nation's first bird sanctuary.*

a small bundle of commitment who, as an Audubon volunteer and warden, has for many decades placed her powerboat and educational message between the pelicans and those who would harm them. In 1987, she helped the refuge capture forty young pelicans from the island she had been protecting, and brought to them to San Bernard National Wildlife Refuge's Cedar Lake unit to establish a second rookery. The birds tried to nest but after few years, storms flooded their nests, and they didn't immediately return. In the meantime, for the price of a pickup truck the refuge purchased badly eroding Dressing Point Island at nearby Big Boggy National Wildlife Refuge. They riprapped the shoreline, planted stabilizing grasses, and the brown pelicans returned to join almost twelve thousand other nesting colonial birds. From here they expanded to Cedar Lake, where pelicans now often stand in line to nest on the five secluded islands in the shallow bay.

Paul Kroegel's passion provided an auspicious beginning for the National Wildlife Refuge System, for most have begun and grown, like Pelican Island, through the efforts of private citizens and employees who have cared. ☙

low-lying shrubs and beaches of the Chandeleur Islands, which form a dynamic barrier along the Gulf of Mexico coast. In 1963, the brown pelican was extinct in Louisiana. An aggressive reintroduction program brought almost one hundred Florida juveniles to the refuge's North Island. From this modest beginning, the population recently peaked at sixteen thousand birds. Vigilant monitoring and habitat improvements help maintain this important population.

The islands are constantly reshaped by wind, storms, and tidal action, and are vulnerable to catastrophes. In 1998, a single hurricane eliminated 80 percent of the barrier islands and half of the nesting pelican population. A three-year banding study is shedding light on where the pelicans are breeding while the refuge habitat recovers. The staff also works closely with the Army Corps of Engineers, which is using dredge spoil from its projects to reinforce refuge islands that might otherwise require fifteen years to reform.

A modern-day Paul Kroegel has been the guardian of another Pelican Island in Corpus Christi Bay, for many years Texas's only brown pelican colony. Her name is Emilie Payne,

when the birds were finally listed as endangered. Two years later, DDT and other pesticides were banned as the cause of the eggshell thinning. In time, brown pelicans became the first species affected by pesticide poisoning to make a comeback.

Today's refuge guardians are facing different challenges. Wave action could completely erode the tiny island, now barely two acres, in just fifty years. Rising sea levels threaten to engulf it. The refuge and volunteers have placed an oyster shell berm around the island to slow the process, and planted native grasses and trees in hopes of stabilizing the shoreline. Elsewhere on the refuge they've bulldozed and burned non-native vegetation threatening the native mangroves, live oaks, and cabbage palms that birds use for nesting, foraging, and roosting. The nation's first refuge is a fitting symbol: although not every refuge requires this level of management, many do and the devotion to stewardship here is mirrored throughout the Refuge System.

A different ocean laps the shores of Breton Island (Louisiana), the nation's second refuge. The highest nesting population of brown pelicans in North America nest on the

FLORIDA PANTHER

He is called catamount, puma, cougar, or mountain lion, depending on the region of the country. In Florida, the big, tawny cat is the Florida panther, a subspecies that once roamed throughout the southeastern United States. Limited today to South Florida, panthers are nocturnal and masters of stealth and secrecy, posing challenges for those who wish to study and restore them.

Loss of habitat is the most significant threat to the survival of this species. The 26,400-acre Florida Panther National Wildlife Refuge was established for the imperiled cat, which needs a lot of space. A female requires seventy to eighty square miles; a male, sometimes more than two hundred square miles. The refuge provides habitat for about five to twelve cats at any one time.

Numbering less than one hundred today, the Florida panther remains one of the most endangered of North American species. This animal is at the top of the food chain and is an important barometer of the environment's health. Scores of species, from black bear and zebra-tailed butterflies to rare orchids, rely on the same habitat, which also soaks up more than fifty-five inches of rain per year and helps purify the water that South Floridians drink.

◁ ◁ ◁ ◁ *A nervous, captive-reared red wolf parent provides just a shimmering glimpse as it ghosts through the forest.*

◁ ◁ *Much of the red wolf recovery is occurring on refuges. To expand the Alligator River (North Carolina) population, young wolf pups have been relocated to Mattamuskeet and Pocosin Lakes, two nearby refuges. Breeding adults have been placed on secluded islands at Cape Romain (South Carolina) and St. Vincent (Florida).*

◁ *A handful of Florida panthers and some relocated from Texas are the nucleus of a recovery program that is inching forward.*

△ At Ding Darling National Wildlife Refuge (Florida), roseate spoonbills forage before leaving for their night roosts high in the trees. These dramatic birds with spatulalike bills are postcard material, forming streamers of pink as they fan out across the marsh. This sanctuary, located on the edge of a bustling urban area, reduces disturbance and handles high visitation with its auto tour and stunning visitor center. J. N. "Ding" Darling, early chief of the Bureau of Biological Survey, could foresee the real estate potential of the area and worked to establish Sanibel Island as a refuge. It was renamed in his honor in 1978.

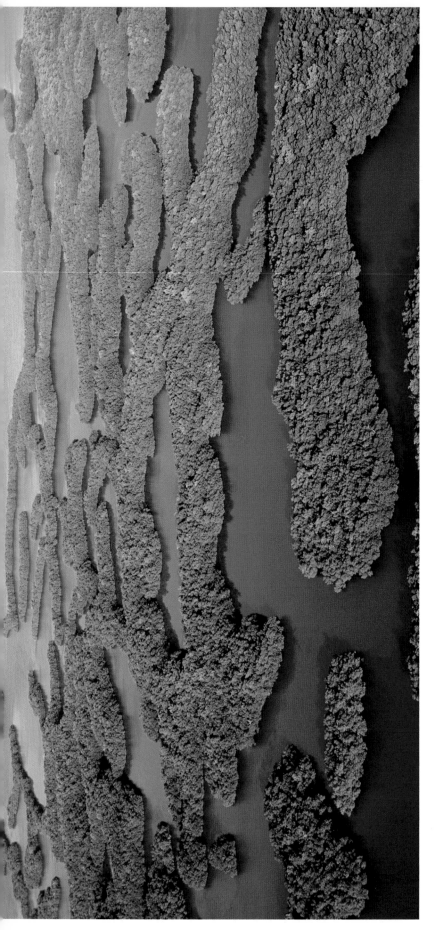

△ Two hundred species of fish inhabit the briny water at Ten Thousand Islands National Wildlife Refuge (Florida), an important coastal nursery for marine fish and a sanctuary for endangered West Indian manatees and three species of sea turtles. ▷ The manatee, or sea cow, weighs up to one ton and is native to Florida, the Caribbean, and parts of South America. Florida's Crystal River was established to protect these endangered marine mammals. ▷ ▷ In 1980, local citizens helped to establish Tensas National Wildlife Refuge (Louisiana) in the Mississippi Valley to preserve a 66,325-acre swath of forest—just in time to help save the threatened Louisiana black bear. Anticipating the time it will be recaptured for relocation to another refuge, researchers measure and assess the health of a bear lured into a culvert trap.

SPECIES WATCH

WEST INDIAN MANATEE

Upon close inspection, the mermaid Captain Christopher Columbus thought he saw on the Gulf Coast in 1493 had no luscious curves, only a large body, tough hairy skin, and a short broad tail. The one-ton marine mammal was the West Indian manatee, or sea cow, native to Florida, the Caribbean, and parts of South America.

The shy, peaceful manatees like basking just under the surface of the water, which must be warmer than 68 degrees for them to survive. Perfect conditions for manatees exist at Florida's spring-fed Kings Bay, also a popular recreation area. Speeding boats and scuba divers disturb the curious manatees and can separate mothers and calves. The backs of many animals bear gashes and scars from repeated propeller strikes, and watercraft accidents account for 80 percent of human-caused manatee deaths.

They were declared endangered in 1967, and thirteen years later the citizens of Citrus County raised enough money for The Nature Conservancy to protect twenty small, undeveloped islands in the bay. These were purchased by the Fish and Wildlife Service in 1983 to become Crystal River National Wildlife Refuge. The refuge now shelters 20 percent of the nation's manatees, sometimes up to 150 animals, and is helping to build their numbers through speed limits, closed zones, an aggressive education program, and vigilant refuge and volunteer patrols.

Alligator

In the early 1900s, hunters descended in record numbers upon Okefenokee, the Everglades, and other southern wetlands to stalk a reptile descended from dinosaurs. Profit-hungry swampers traveled dim waterways in canoes, shining a headlamp to locate the glowing red eyes of an alligator. Others stood in the shallows, grunting into a long, hollow tube to lure a big one into their revolver's range. In an instant, a half-submerged log could awaken to bellow its rage, becoming a killing machine of amazing speed with armorlike hide and a row of locking, razor-sharp teeth. Old tales describe alligators twenty feet long, weighing a half ton. In 1906, a big gator skin could be sold for $1.50. Much like the era's colonial birds, which fueled the millinery trade, thousands of alligators died to become fashionable shoes, belts, and handbags around the world.

Once an emblem of the swamp, the alligator all but disappeared. Its existence was so doubtful that in 1967 the alligator was listed as endangered. Refuges and other natural areas began to actively manage habitat for them. Hunting was banned and the Fish and Wildlife Service cracked down on illegal commercial trade of their skins. These efforts produced fast results and, in one decade, they began rebounding on their own. The keys, say most researchers, are protecting their wetland habitat, studying their habits, and leaving them alone. The favor is returned, for it is now clear that providing a sanctuary for the alligator also preserves the integrity of the swamp. Despite human efforts to dam and drain southern swamps, the alligator remains their prime architect. They plow through impassable areas. They excavate trails and small pools that create openings and form travel corridors used by many other species. They reproduce prolifically, and regulate their own numbers: the males will not hesitate to kill each other, or their own young.

96

When summer water levels drop throughout the Southeast, alligators also become the unbidden allies of colonial nesting birds. Arthur R. Marshall Loxahatchee National Wildlife Refuge protects 147,000 acres of Everglades habitat and associated wetlands. This bonanza of birds helps feed thirty thousand alligators, one of the largest populations in the refuge copes with invasive species and water-quality problems from agricultural and urban runoff. They also work with the Army Corps of Engineers and Southern Florida Water Management District to time and control swamp water levels to mimic seasonal cycles, allowing natural processes to endure. During the summer drawdown, the refuge assures that a mosaic of pools remain for wildlife. The gators wiggle and thrash, enlarging these shallow depressions, often in the shadow of the nesting colonies. The little gator holes concentrate fish within easy reach of tens of thousands of nesting birds and their young. The fish also breed here, guaranteeing food for another generation of birds, young alligators, and others. Opportunistic alligators occasionally snatch birds that fall from the nest but more often keep marauding raccoons from doing greater damage to the rookery.

As many as eight hundred thousand waterfowl funnel down the Central and Mississippi flyways, concentrating on Lacassine's (Louisiana) sixteen-thousand-acre impoundment in heavily developed southern Florida. To preserve the swamp, the South. Each year, researchers fly aerial surveys, easily locating the female's conspicuous three-foot high nesting mound of soil and vegetation. She lays and carefully covers twenty to fifty eggs, trusting the heat from the decaying matter to incubate them for two months while she attends the nest. When she hears the chirping sounds of her young ones, she bites off the top of the mound to free them. She is surprisingly tender. Even though her jaws are strong enough to crush a turtle's shell, she mouths each unhatched egg, gently rolls it against her hard pallet until it opens, then leads her hatchlings to the water. After each egg is checked, she leads her hatchlings to the water. Aerial researchers will note the open nest and soon capture, tag, and examine some of the young. Research is a vital part of alligator management at Lacassine and other refuges, where scientists study

everything from hatchlings to battle-scarred patriarchs, documenting nesting success, population health, and more.

In 1987, only twenty years after its listing, the alligator was considered fully recovered and was delisted. Although some recent die-offs and cases of infertility are affecting a few central Florida populations, there are now millions of alligators from Oklahoma and eastern Texas through the Gulf states, and north to the Carolinas. Almost twenty national wildlife refuges have played a significant role in providing a sanctuary, helping to rescue a species most known for its treacherous bite, from the jaws of extinction. ↵

△ *Lying placidly like a half-submerged log, the American alligator's menace is hard to see. Beneath the seeming torpor are lethal jaws propelled by ancient instinct along with surprising speed and agility. Once endangered, their numbers are now stable at Okefenokee National Wildlife Refuge (Georgia and Florida) and throughout the South, where protection and sanctuary have guided their comeback.*

▽ *Baby alligators often cling to their mother's head and back as she travels, providing the youngsters with protection from predators.*

Jack Watson

Native only to a few islands off the south Florida coast, the smallest deer in North America was struggling for survival and needed a giant-sized protector. They found one in Jack Watson, the big, cigar-chomping defender sent by the Fish and Wildlife Service in 1951 to rid the islands of poachers and meat hunters who were decimating the deer.

There were so few Key deer remaining that Watson patrolled in a vehicle, on foot, and in boats for a full year before he finally saw his first. This man who wouldn't hesitate to shoot a resistant poacher's boat full of holes was smitten. He relentlessly pursued poachers and began to see more deer, some outpacing his motorboat as they swam between islands. He felt sorry for the swimming deer and once tried to lift a small buck into his boat. The feisty animal struggled and kicked so hard the chagrined and battered Watson immediately returned him to the water.

In his free time, Watson made detailed observations of the deer's habitat, forced people to chain up free-roaming dogs, rehabilitated injured deer, and occasionally arrested people for trapping songbirds or bagging a great white heron for their Thanksgiving dinner. He claimed that the local judge, having once been caught on a Watson stakeout, was sympathetic to his cases and trusted his prosecution of violators.

He cultivated widespread respect, getting many people to lease their property as a temporary sanctuary and eventually sell it to establish the National Key Deer Refuge in 1957. There were barely twenty-five deer when Watson became the first manager, but over several decades, he nurtured that small legacy to several hundred. Today, six hundred deer are thriving on the refuge.

Key Deer

Where other species have succumbed to the crush of development, this plucky little deer has not only survived, it has thrived. Even though houses are stacked up against the refuge boundaries, and roads crisscross their habitat, the key deer has adapted, with help from generations of Fish and Wildlife Service defenders and others who have protected them from harm.

When the smallest deer in North America teetered on the brink of extinction in their only home on the Florida Keys, it seemed fitting that the U.S. Bureau of Biological Survey, the precursor to the Fish and Wildlife Service, would send a giant to rescue them. Jack Watson's stature and no-nonsense reputation matched his desire to help the struggling deer, a twenty-year job that involved nabbing poachers, warming neighbors to the idea of a sanctuary, and helping to establish and manage a refuge for them.

The battle occurred in the Florida Keys, a subtropical island paradise curving along the southern tip of Florida. These worn down coral reefs topped with limestone deposits sustain incredible plant and wildlife diversity, even though only a few have fresh water. Four national wildlife refuges protect a wealth of jungle plants and wildlife that include twenty-two threatened and endangered species—more than any other national wildlife refuge. Five species are found nowhere else on earth, including the Key deer, a white-tailed deer barely as tall as a big collie that occurs only on the National Key Deer Refuge. Here, another generation browses on mangroves, sips water from limestone reservoirs, and learns how to cope with traffic and curious people.

In the 1940s, Jim Silver, director of the Bureau's southeastern region, had heard that only seventy Key deer could be found. Many had been killed for meat when the Overseas Railroad was built. Poachers used dogs or set fires to force the deer into the water, where partners waiting in boats clubbed them to death. Lacking a budget and authority to help the deer, he took up his pen, writing that " . . . the most unique deer in the U.S. is still hanging on to a precarious existence. . . ."

His reports generated national compassion and action, even from the Bureau's former first chief, J. N. "Ding" Darling, whose 1941 syndicated cartoon depicting poachers in boats killing the tiny deer hit newspapers across the nation. In 1951, with deer reduced to just a few islands, hunters in the Boone and Crockett Club committed a year's salary and expenses to hire a warden to stop the poachers. That man was a Fish and Wildlife Service employee named Jack Watson. When funds ran out, the National Wildlife Federation picked up the tab for several years.

Through Watson's vigilance, poachers and market hunters were routed out. For the deer to survive the south Florida's burgeoning development, they needed a place of their own. The deer had many supporters, though few wanted to sell their land for a refuge. In 1954, Congress finally passed a bill that included authority for the Fish and Wildlife Service to lease lands from willing landowners and manage for the deer. Seven thousand acres were eventually leased at a dollar per acre, forming an unofficial refuge in the nick of time.

Overhunting and loss of habitat continued to take a toll; only twenty-five deer could be found in 1957, when the refuge was finally established. Watson became the first refuge manager. Working eighteen-hour days, he pushed for endangered species protection in 1967, purchased land for a permanent refuge from willing sellers, and left a legacy of commitment that has grown with the population.

There are now about six hundred Key deer, perhaps the maximum the refuge can currently sustain. Refuge monitoring and studies show the deer are healthy, with high fawn survival. The deer swim back and forth among twenty-six islands, though most remain on Big Pine and No Name keys, the only two that offer year-round habitat and reliable fresh water. Because of their concentration on these two islands, the staff worries that disease or a hurricane could wipe out almost the entire herd. On some of the outlying islands they are developing new water sources, removing nonnative plants, and completing prescribed burns to sweeten the landscape with fresh young growth. Their hope is to buy a little insurance by dispersing the deer to safeguard this hard-won recovery.

Today a deer nibbling on a mangrove might be a stone's throw from people walking on the beach. The sounds of bistro music and car traffic mix with the rutting calls of bucks. The Florida Key deer are an enigma. Where other species have succumbed to the crush of development, this plucky little deer has not only survived, it has thrived. Even though houses are stacked up against the refuge boundaries, and roads crisscross their habitat, the Key deer has adapted, with help from generations of Fish and Wildlife Service defenders and others who have protected them from harm. ⌐

△ *Face, antlers, hoofed feet . . . everything is diminutive on the Florida Key deer. Just over two feet high, North America's smallest deer was once savagely slaughtered for food and sport. It has made a solid comeback at Florida's National Key Deer Refuge.*

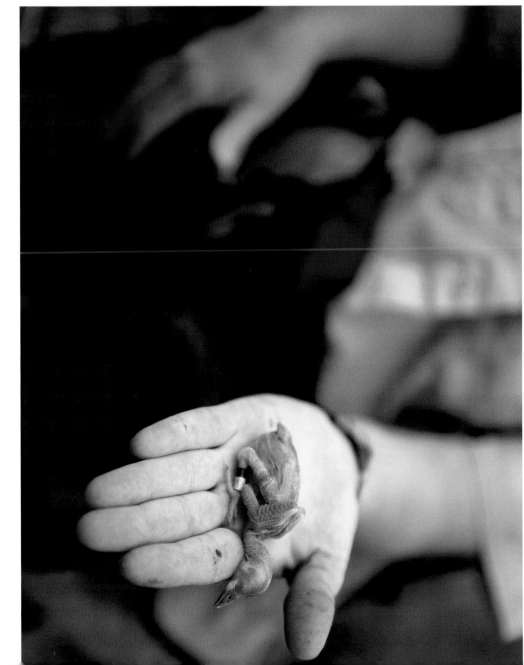

△ △ The Suwannee River snakes through the Okefenokee Swamp, where more than 396,000 acres are protected within the national wildlife refuge. The swamp is a place of sharp contrasts, where darkness and mystery exist next to beauty and unspoiled wilderness, where faint whisperings are pierced by the bellow of an alligator and where prodigal plants abide and a myriad of creatures that crawl, swim, and fly abound.

△ and ▽ Some animals' habitat requirements are very specific. The endangered red-cockaded woodpecker requires open stands of southern pines at least eighty years old, with nesting cavities. Loss of habitat has spurred ingenuity: many now nest in human-made metal nesting holes sealed into suitable trees on southern national wildlife refuges. The palm-sized young are weighed and measured by refuge researchers who monitor the nests.

▷ *A snowy egret shows off elegant nuptial plumage, the reason so many were slaughtered in the late 1800s and early 1900s.*

▷ ▷ *Roseate spoonbills clack their bills as part of an ancient and enthusiastic breeding dance. The pairing is sealed when a stick offered by the male is accepted by his mate.*

102

Courtship is a colorful and public drama, where glossy ibises glide in slow, circular flights; roseate spoonbills carry branches to their mates; and flamingoes lavishly preen their rose-hued feathers.

Colonial Birds

During two walks in Manhattan in 1886 Frank Chapman, an ornithologist at the American Museum of Natural History, is said to have counted at least forty species of birds. Showy breeding plumage was everywhere. The experienced birder did not sight the birds in trees or on the wing but identified them from feathers adorning hundreds of women's hats. Feathers were in vogue and some of the most coveted were long, elegant heron feathers and lavish nuptial plumes of snowy egrets.

These continued extravagances enraged Chapman and many others, who prevailed upon President Theodore Roosevelt to establish the first bird sanctuary at Pelican Island in 1903 to save its nesting brown pelicans. From that first act, a system of lands was born that places the needs of wildlife first.

Pelicans, egrets, herons, ibises, and other colonial birds are especially vulnerable to humans because they gather in tightly-packed, large colonies to breed and nest. Courtship is a colorful and public drama, where glossy ibises glide in slow, circular flights; roseate spoonbills carry branches to their mates; and flamingoes lavishly preen their rose-hued feathers. From coast to coast, they nest together in trees, bushes, shrubs, and on the ground, preferring islands and other secluded habitat that provide a nearby meal and help deter predators.

In Florida's Everglades, protecting their nesting requirements is an act of partnership. A pristine corner of this great tropical swamp is preserved at Arthur R. Marshall Loxahatchee National Wildlife Refuge. Some years up to twenty thousand white ibis, cattle egrets, anhingas, little blue and tricolored herons, and others jam nests onto isolated tree islands in the northern Everglades. These spring nuptial rites usually occur just as the Army Corps of Engineers and

Southern Florida Water Management District are drawing down water in anticipation of torrential summer rain. The refuge staff closely monitors nesting and the receding water, relying on a sympathetic partnership with the Corps and District to coordinate a slow drawdown so pockets of water remain near the bird colonies.

Halfway across the country, grassy islands and pothole marshes at Chase Lake (North Dakota) make a dramatic backdrop for up to half of the world's population of nesting American white pelicans. These stunning white birds with a ten-foot wingspan used to be found at marshes and lakes throughout the West, but the steady loss of wetlands has

concentrated them almost exclusively on national wildlife refuges. From fewer than fifty in 1908, when Chase Lake was set aside for them, white pelican numbers have soared to a recent high of thirty-five thousand. Most of the refuge is a designated Wilderness Area, a nearly roadless landscape providing added protection for a world's treasure.

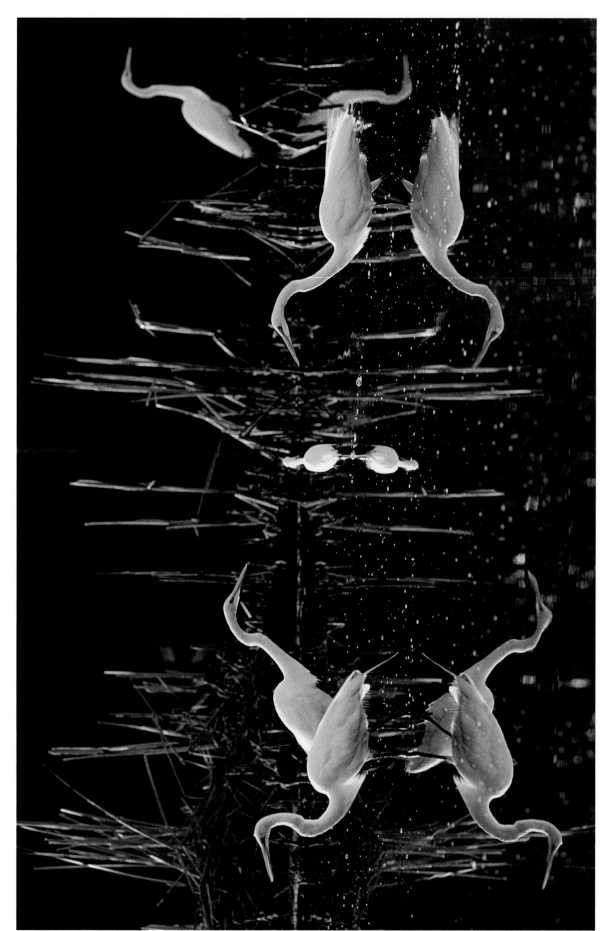

Ohio's West Sister National Wildlife Refuge, a seventy-seven-acre island Wilderness Area on Lake Erie, sustains the largest heron, egret, and cormorant rookery in the United States Great Lakes. Nesting numbers of black-crowned night herons have slowly declined because young trees and brushy plants needed for nest sites are being replaced by older forest. For decades, wilderness designation has eliminated disturbance but now challenges refuge managers because it prohibits use of machinery to create a younger, more open forest. To produce the necessary habitat and save an investment spanning decades, the refuge staff travels miles by boat and relies on two-person saws, axes, and other hand tools powered by dedication and sweat.

A century ago, the first refuge wardens defended colonial birds with shotguns and a few trespass signs. Today thousands of Blue Goose signs protect rookeries across the nation and refuge staffs have relinquished threatening guns for a bigger arsenal of laws, education, and management tools. They shield storm-ravaged islands with plant barriers to slow erosion, replant trees to replace old timers that have fallen, clear brush off of sandy nesting sites, remove predators to give youngsters a better chance, and buy a few more acres of marsh to expand the refuge buffer. These guardians have guaranteed colonial birds a place of refuge to dance on air and answer the ancient call that is their birthright, and our legacy. ✍

△ Tall, conspicuously white, and covered with elegant feathers, great egrets foraging in the marsh or sitting on a nest had no chance against well-armed hunters who supplied plumes for the fashion industry. Many of the earliest refuges were established to protect egrets, herons, and other harried birds. Nests that were barren a century ago are now flourishing at southern refuges, from Pinckney Island (South Carolina) to Noxubee (Mississippi).

▷ Dragonflies are the helicopters of the insect world, using their double set of wings to hover — this one converting a pond lily to a landing pad. Dragonflies, other less-celebrated creatures, and plants are vital components of a healthy ecosystem. Early refuges were often established to preserve a single species, while today, many refuges are charged to preserve, restore, and manage entire ecosystems.

American Deserts

In summer it is a vast, arid landscape — a place of faded pinks and muted browns, weathered outposts and withered waterways. It is a hostile place, where wrinkled lava flows meet sawtooth mountains, and arroyo plants bristle with piercing thorns. When daytime temperatures exceed 110 degrees it can be 180 degrees on the ground. Even so, a rich array of plants and animals have adapted to this sometimes unforgiving environment. Agile bighorn sheep ascend steep precipices, finding rainwater in stone water basins called tinajas. The cactus wren may find a cool microclimate in the shade of a prickly pear pad. Mice, gophers, tortoises, and other excavators build extensive underground burrows to escape the unrelenting heat.

American deserts receive just inches of rain each year, which barely revive the parched land. The rain is usually gentle, but desert storms can assault with sudden fury, dumping several inches in a few hours. This onslaught recharges perennial stream oases where the deer and coyote find water and songbirds nest. It floods and

△ *From a distance, rocky ridges and rugged desert canyons often seem devoid of life. Were it not for the occasional flash of a white rump patch, bighorn sheep might go unnoticed, blending naturally with the faded browns of the desert landscape. A bighorn ram has spotted a group of ewes and lambs, which band up and move to the point of a ridge. The ram follows the nervous group, looking for ewes that are ready to mate.*

soaks the thirsty soil, replenishing frugal cacti and leaving a bonanza of blossoms across the gently sloped bajadas and flat washes. After a heavy rain, desert mirages turn into real seasonal marshes that remain a few months, serving as vital stopovers for thousands of migratory ducks, geese, sandhill cranes, and other waterbirds.

Water from an underground river, seeps, and sinkholes may taste acrid at Bitter Lake (New Mexico), but it supports a bounty of birds, frogs, fish, and wildlife found at few other places. Nevada's Stillwater refuge must purchase water, then closely time and manage flooding and drawdowns through miles of human-made structures. California's Salton Sea water is becoming more saline from agricultural runoff. The refuge has convened a working group of stakeholders, scientists, and others to help find ways to rehabilitate this ailing ecosystem so vital to birds.

Deserts or desertlike land cover nearly one-third of the earth's land surface. The North American desert, the fifth largest in the world, includes the Great Basin, Mojave, Sonoran, and Chihuahuan deserts. Though each of these desert habitats occur at different elevations, they share common geological forces and land forms, such as washes, sand dunes, and dry lake beds. Two dozen national wildlife refuges preserve these desert ecosystems in eastern Oregon, California, Nevada, Arizona, New Mexico, and Texas.

The desert is a tortured land racked by earthquakes and scarred by volcanic eruptions. Its anatomy lies exposed where gravelly washes bear evidence of ancient shorelines, sea fossils, glacial waters, or vast inland lakes. The earth is cracked with fissures by drought and may be fractured by caves, tunnels, and rifts. Insistent wind and water forces over time to gnaw at mountain ridges, leaving great ruts, narrow canyons, and smoothed surfaces that shine with a time-honed varnish. Water often leaves surface minerals in its wake, forming a white alkali veneer that can extend for miles. Wind-sculpted dunes can be hundreds of feet deep.

The lack of rainfall in deserts is compounded by temperatures that can vary fifty degrees in a day. Desert plants and wildlife have developed unusual ways of coping with the climate and storing or conserving water. The seeds of annual plants often lie dormant until just the right conditions allow them to germinate and flower. Some plants can

△ *A classic view of Sonoran desert cactus in late spring includes the saguaro cactus—the hallmark of this desert—along with a spindly ocotillo ablaze in colorful blossoms and the prickly cholla.*

▽ *The craggy Castle Dome Mountains at Kofa National Wildlife Refuge (Arizona) are a major stronghold for bighorn sheep, a Mexican subspecies native to the southeastern Sonoran desert of Arizona and Mexico.*

Frugal cacti have a thick cuticle that seals in moisture. A large saguaro can store a ton or more of water. Even though needle-sharp hairs protect its tough skin, many are pockmarked with holes made by birds and other animals probing for moisture.

endure for years without reseeding or coaxing. The protective covering on seeds and pods protect them from the heat, but can be cracked by teeth and bills designed to open them. Prudent cacti have a thick cuticle that seals in surplus water; a giant saguaro can soak up a ton of water a day, and store as much as eight tons. The needle-sharp thorns, or hairs, on these succulent plants help protect them from solar radiation and predators. Leaves, or the lack of them, also help conserve water.

Tracks in the sand, nests among the thorns, and symmetrically shaped mounds are evidence of animals that have adjusted to these uncompromising conditions. Pronghorn antelope thrive at Sheldon-Hart (Oregon) and Buenos Aires (Arizona) national wildlife refuges, their hollow hair helping to insulate them from both heat and cold. As the temperature drops, snakes and lizards regulate their temperature by moving between hot and cool locations or changing the color of their skin. Desert tortoises at Kofa (Arizona) and Pahranagat (Nevada) make burrows up to thirty feet deep in the loose soil, sleeping away the cold winter and

avoiding the intense summer heat. Their hard carapaces (shells) conserve moisture and protect them from sunburn and piercing thorns. Some frogs and butterflies just wait, sometimes for years, until favorable conditions occur before emerging.

No matter how each animal conserves moisture, they know where it is concealed. Jack rabbits and birds bite into the heavily pleated saguaro and the flattened prickly pear to suck precious moisture from these desert sponges. Deer paw to find underground springs and bighorn sheep, burros, and quail find a few precious swallows in mountain tinajas.

Because food and water are scarce in the desert, vast space is required to sustain wildlife diversity. Three of the largest refuges in the Lower 48, Desert (Nevada), Cabeza Prieta (Arizona), and Kofa (Arizona) National Wildlife Refuges together protect more than three million acres; the latter two include vast expanses of designated wilderness.

While protecting habitat as a refuge is enough for many desert species, some of our most imperiled desert creatures require a helping hand. During periods of drought, desert bighorn sheep populations might collapse were it not for artificial water collection basins built by people. Thinning creosote and providing well water when rainfall is sparse at Cabeza Prieta will allow young greens to prosper to feed the dwindling Sonoran pronghorn. At Desert, natural springs and a hatchery are safeguarding Pahrump poolfish saved from a private ranch near Las Vegas.

Sevilleta National Wildlife Refuge, located in the New Mexico desert, is a national center for research. Its Spanish translation, "the place where the edges meet," describes how snowcapped mountains, clad with pinyon pine and juniper forests, transition to playa marshes, the arid Chihuahuan desert, and the high elevation Great Basin desert. The roots of partnership flourish in this desert setting. The Campbell Family Foundation, anxious to revive their 230,000 acres after years of overgrazing, sold it to The Nature Conservancy in 1973 for $500,000, a fraction of its value. As has been the case with numerous other refuges, the Conservancy turned over management of what would become the seventh-largest refuge in the Lower 48 to the Fish and Wildlife Service, to manage as part of the National Wildlife Refuge System. Since then, the refuge has restored the overgrazed land to a more natural condition. It has also maintained the foundation's mission of research. The refuge includes a Mexican wolf captive management facility that acclimates this endangered species to its native habitat before reintroduction to other sites. Desert bighorn sheep have been released here to restore historic populations. Scientists from around the nation routinely conduct ongoing studies: Sevilleta is the only national wildlife refuge to serve as one of twenty-one Long Term Ecological Research Project locations.

Much like the great Alaskan wilderness, deserts are untamed landscapes, where intimacy and grandeur occur side by side. A spring shower can suddenly emblazon an isolated gully with showy blooms, some lasting but a single day. A sunset subdues a sprawling range of craggy peaks into soft silhouettes veiled in evening lilac. The desert's austere beauty is an emblem of solitude and wildness. Its preservation on millions of acres of national wildlife refuges is a celebration of ancient adaptation and rugged survival. 🐾

▽ *Malheur National Wildlife Refuge (Oregon) is rich with the history of wagon trains, cattle drives, famous ranches, and diverse wildlife populations tied to its high desert habitat. Each spring, greater sage-grouse gather on large areas protected by the refuge, called leks, where the males parade in hopes of impressing a mate. The male fans his spiky tail feathers and rapidly inflates and deflates air sacs on his chest, which make a loud, booming sound. His life is inextricably linked to sagebrush, which provides cover for nesting, shelter from bad weather, and serves as much of his diet.*
▷ *A rocky basaltic ledge is first a theater for lavish prairie falcon courtship displays and later, the base for their bulky nest. Prairie falcons are common at Sheldon National Wildlife Refuge (Nevada), where trees and rocky outcrops offer perches for hunting the tablelands below.*

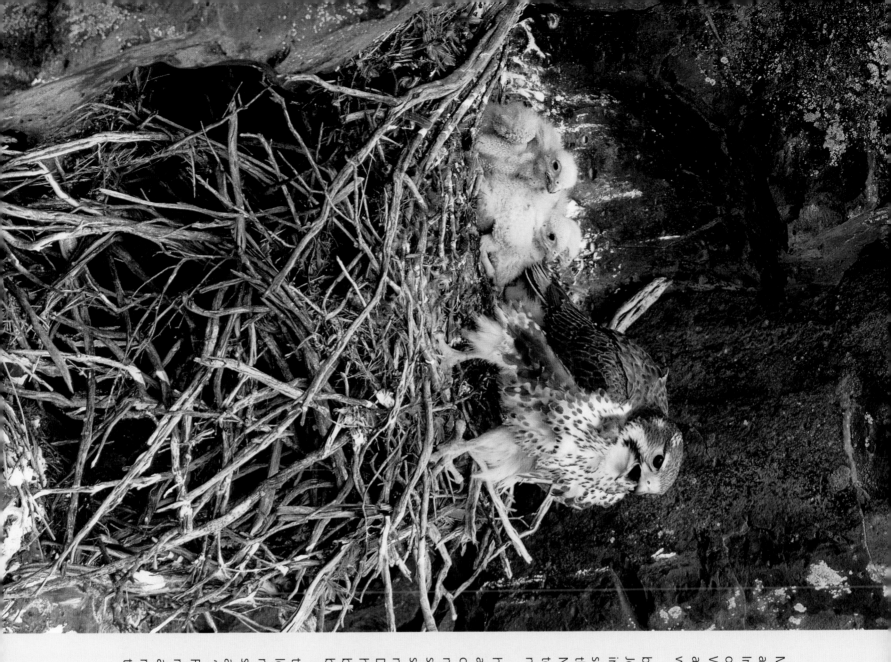

Pete Dunne

Many people know Pete Dunne as a prolific author, the vice president of Natural History Information for the New Jersey Audubon Society, or the editor of *New Jersey Audubon Magazine*. While Dunne wears all of these hats, he is first a naturalist with a powerful appreciation for wild America.

National wildlife refuges have been in his blood since he was in his twenties living in New Jersey. "I recall being twenty-four years old, wanting to become a birder and a known quantity, searching for purpose and identity. I would walk the roads to the Wilderness Area of Great Swamp National Wildlife Refuge two or three times a week to develop my skills, and to gain the nurturing that nature provides."

On his travels across the nation he has visited hundreds of refuges, some evoking strong images and memories. Bosque del Apache (New Mexico) combines the unlikely opposites of desert and marsh. Seney (Michigan) elicits the perfume and serenity of the north woods. Rio Grande (Texas) showcases life on the edge, where land and gulf meet. And the prairie pothole gem Des Lacs (North Dakota), he recalls fondly, was located next to a highway where he happened to spot three life list birds—the white pelican, Wilson's phalarope, and black tern—while he was laboring to fix a flat tire.

Every Monday Dunne shares his wit, observation skills, and birding lore on a morning walk he leads at the Cape May Bird Observatory, located near Cape May National Wildlife Refuge. He can see a half dozen birds on the hike that were almost extinct a hundred years ago. He reflects, "Something as ambitious as a National Wildlife Refuge is not a frivolous thing. A century ago our natural endowment was being paupered. Refuges are a key component [in preserving this legacy], a model to be emulated. For people, they are places that nurture intimacy and a bond with nature."

△ A desert bighorn sheep lamb follows its mother at Desert National Wildlife Refuge (Nevada), scampering across steep slabs of rock and jumping down gravel drainages with the same surefooted agility as an adult. Bighorn rest and forage only where visibility is good, relying on extraordinary eyesight and keen hearing to avoid mountain lions, coyotes, eagles, and other predators. ▷ The muscled form and massive, curved horns of a desert bighorn ram are an unforgettable sight, a striking emblem of desert tenacity and survival.

Bighorn Sheep

A desert bighorn ram picks his way across a granite slope, turning massive curled horns scarred by battles and time toward a sound carried by the wind. The desert sprawls thousands of feet below in a soft purple haze, layers of basins and washes, sloped bajadas and ranges, joined in an endless horizon. Alert, he watches, then bounds with economical grace from his rocky outpost up the steep ascent, finding footholds no human eye can see. He is the lord of the mountains in a desert realm known for the tyranny of its climate, prickly vegetation, and unforgiving terrain.

Names of canyons, springs, and other desert landmarks often capture an area's oral history and lore. Arizona's Aqua Dulce Mountains were named for their hidden caches of water. The Sheep Mountains in southern Nevada harken to a time of plenty and place where bighorn sheep could be found. Their domain was reduced to little more than a name on a map in 1936, when the Desert National Wildlife Range was established to protect bighorn sheep habitat. Throughout the West, desert bighorn sheep populations had plummeted due to market hunting, competition with livestock, and exposure to livestock diseases. Some populations were immediately lost to these stresses; others slowly declined and became vulnerable to predation, injuries, and the strain of drought.

Sprawling over 1.5 million acres, Desert is the largest refuge in the Lower 48 states. It preserves the Southwest's largest intact block of desert bighorn sheep habitat, and perhaps North America's largest bighorn sheep population, now fluctuating between eight hundred and fifteen hundred animals.

In a region with four to fifteen inches of annual rainfall, water is the lifeblood of wildlife. During a good year, rain or snowmelt spurs the growth of lush vegetation,

reducing the period when bighorns require water. The small, porous sedimentary rock basins in Desert's mountains are capable of storing water only for a short period. As temperatures soar with the onset of summer, both the moisture-bearing forage and basins dry up.

Even though the wandering bighorns can survive a week without drinking, a struggling population can succumb to drought in a single season or two. When bighorn sheep populations were failing, refuges and other wildlife agencies began building human-made water catchments to provide water during times of drought. Over the years Desert has improved thirty-four natural springs and built twenty-seven rainwater catchments, each located with care to provide vital sources of summer water across six mountain ranges. Most were financed by conservation groups and built with hand tools wielded by volunteers committed to the bighorns and undaunted by the desert environment.

In order to help restore desert bighorn sheep populations in the West, surplus animals were captured for relocation. An evolution in capture methods and success has occurred, from early trappers who caught bighorns in padded leg-hold traps and attached bells to their necks to modern-day capture specialists who shoot immobilizing darts or a netgun from a helicopter and affix satellite telemetry collars to follow them.

In the 1940s, a group of captive bighorns was established to produce relocation stock at Desert's Corn Creek unit, where they remained for two decades. The little band never produced a surplus, but were the source of pioneering research on techniques for determining age, lamb survival, and other management challenges. It fell to other sanctuaries, such as Kofa (Arizona), to provide animals for relocation. Since it was established, Kofa has furnished over four hundred desert bighorn sheep for relocations in the Southwest. The refuge tries to maintain a base population of eight hundred sheep, working with the Arizona Game and Fish Department when there are excess to remove.

Bighorn sheep at Cabeza Prieta (Arizona), in the most arid region in the nation, have also made a comeback. The state of Arizona feared that their populations had been decimated, with perhaps as few as fifty remaining near the Mexican border. Boy scouts, state game rangers, and caring

citizens successfully lobbied President Franklin D. Roosevelt, and in 1939 he created both Kofa and Cabeza Prieta to protect these bighorns and their unique Sonoran Desert habitat. The 860,000-acre Cabeza Prieta refuge, known for its towering, deeply-pleated saguaro cactus and endangered Sonoran pronghorn, is the third largest in the Lower 48. Almost all of the refuge is a designated wilderness.

Like other desert sanctuaries, generations of refuge workers have patrolled to stop bighorn poaching, built water catchments, and studied the resources of this surprisingly productive land. In addition to routine surveys, they have also initiated a five-year study to determine how reliant the bighorns are upon the human-made catchments. The refuge maintains eighteen of them, sometimes hauling water during times of drought, despite comments from some wilderness advocates demanding that the practice be stopped. Refuges are places where wildlife comes first, and in a capricious landscape, a population of three hundred to five hundred bighorn sheep is a hard-won victory. For these bighorns and others on national wildlife refuges, human-made catchments, hauled water, and enduring commitment may be all that stands between life and death during seasons of extreme drought. ❧

△ Desert bighorn sheep have evolved to withstand the stresses of an unrelenting desert summer. They can go without water for a week or more, deriving moisture from the food they eat. But they must have water to survive, and during drought years, the desert may provide little. The staff and volunteers at many refuges have solved the problem by creating rainwater catchments that collect the precious rainfall. It is stored in tanks and flows by gravity to a small basin that usually excludes burros, cattle, and other competitive species. Water catchments are often built completely by hand, in extremely remote locations. ▷ Desert tortoises follow predictable seasonal patterns during lives that span a century.

DESERT TORTOISE

Footprints in sand record the passing of a desert tortoise, a creature of such antiquity it is considered a living fossil, as it makes its way to shade. Its domed carapace (shell), scaley skin, and ability to store water from vegetation allow it to survive in one of the world's harshest environments.

Prior to winter, desert tortoises seek long underground burrows, some thirty feet long, capable of housing several hibernating animals. They emerge in March; during spring and summer, those that are mature may breed. Turtles are cold-blooded and regulate their body heat by moving in and out of the sun. They while away the hot summer months by remaining underground, where the temperature may be fifty degrees cooler.

Despite these survival skills, as few as one out of twenty youngsters may survive to reach sexual maturity at fourteen to twenty years of age. Desert tortoises are declining and considered threatened in portions of several southwestern states due to a variety of threats. Livestock compact the earth and trample vegetation they require for food and cover. Energy and mineral development can collapse their burrows. Off-road vehicles and motorcycles hit animals that move too slowly to escape. Illegal shooting and collection are reducing their numbers. And introduced respiratory diseases and predation by ravens are now also taking a toll.

△ A herd of pronghorn races across big sage at Hart Mountain National Antelope Refuge (Oregon). This secluded valley is littered with broken arrow points, worked obsidian pieces, and other evidence of Native people who relied on the pronghorn for food. ▷ When pronghorn populations plummeted in the West, Hart Mountain and Sheldon (Nevada) were established with the help of concerned sportsmen to provide summer and winter habitat for the fastest land mammal in North America. Good years have followed bad, and it is now common to see twin fawns, a sign of a healthy herd and thriving habitat.

AMERICA'S WILDLIFE REFUGES

Pronghorn

Born of lava flows and earthquakes, the serrated ridges and cliffs of Oregon's Hart Mountain loom over broad tablelands and folded canyons that merge in endless horizons. The arid tablelands are topped with grasses and low-lying clusters of gray green sagebrush, the emblem of the high desert. It is a tableau out of the Old West, complete with deserted American Indian villages, abandoned mines, ranchers' line shacks, and herds of grazing pronghorn antelope.

Neither hot summers nor the knifing winds of winter bother the pronghorn, who wears nature's heating and cooling system. The long, hollow hairs of his coat each trap a tiny column of air, locking in warmth or insulating against heat. Sensing movement, he may turn huge dark eyes toward a speck four miles distant. In a heartbeat he bounds, lifting the white hairs on either side of his rump into a bright fan, a flag of alarm visible to nearby pronghorn. Animals line out behind him and soon, they are nothing but a cinnamon-colored streak, each capable of sprinting at speeds reaching sixty miles per hour.

The pronghorn antelope, the only species of its kind in the world, has endured ice ages, dinosaurs, and other changes that shaped the continent. However, neither flared rump patch warnings nor exceptional eyesight could save North America's fastest land mammal from the guns of market hunters and contemptuous stockmen. Before the nation's European settlement, there were perhaps thirty or forty million pronghorn. They had so decreased in 1908 that a handful were relocated from Yellowstone National Park to the National Bison Range (Montana), when the sanctuary was first established. Their numbers continued to wane. By the 1930s, less than twenty thousand remained in Oregon. Miraculously, almost one-quarter of these survived on the isolated sage-covered rangelands and tablelands at Hart Mountain, where water was ample. Recognizing the importance of this fragile stronghold, citizens led by the Order of the Antelope urged President Franklin Delano Roosevelt to protect the area. Hart Mountain National Antelope Range was established in 1937. Other refuges have been established with pronghorn included among their purposes, but Hart Mountain remains the only national wildlife refuge whose sole purpose is to protect the nation's fastest runner.

As springtime greens the landscape, pregnant does drift off in small bands to have their young. Usually, each will have twins. For a week or more they cache their earth-colored fawns in the brush while they feed, trusting that the nearly odorless and motionless youngsters will remain safe from predators. Although pronghorn are strongly associated with sagebrush, they also require the grasses, forbs, and other low-growing herbaceous vegetation that grows between sagebrush plants to survive, especially after fawning.

One hundred years of cattle and domestic sheep grazing and a government policy of dousing wildfires altered the native vegetation at Hart Mountain. Tall, dense sagebrush overshadows the struggling greens and blocks the open vistas required by these sight-oriented animals. The pronghorn shunned these areas as their numbers declined. Simply protecting habitat for the pronghorn was no longer enough. The refuge responded with research, and a prescribed burning program to reduce areas of dense sagebrush and promote the growth of nutritious forbs.

In country where "sage" appears before many species names, the plant has prime importance, so burning sagebrush has sparked some concern. Through careful Fish and Wildlife Service studies, monitoring, and outreach, the refuge is demonstrating to its neighbors and scientists across the country that carefully planned prescribed burns can benefit pronghorn, sage-grouse, and countless other species. They have also initiated trendsetting studies on the effects of coyote predation during the first crucial weeks of fawning.

No other refuge has devoted so much effort toward habitat restoration, research, and monitoring programs for this fleet-footed species. Over time this singular focus has paid off: bad winters, poor fawn survival, or high predation have, at times, nearly eliminated other pronghorn populations, but Hart Mountain's isolated herd has endured and now thrives, a safety valve for pronghorn in its region and the refuge, a lasting guardian for the nation. ✍

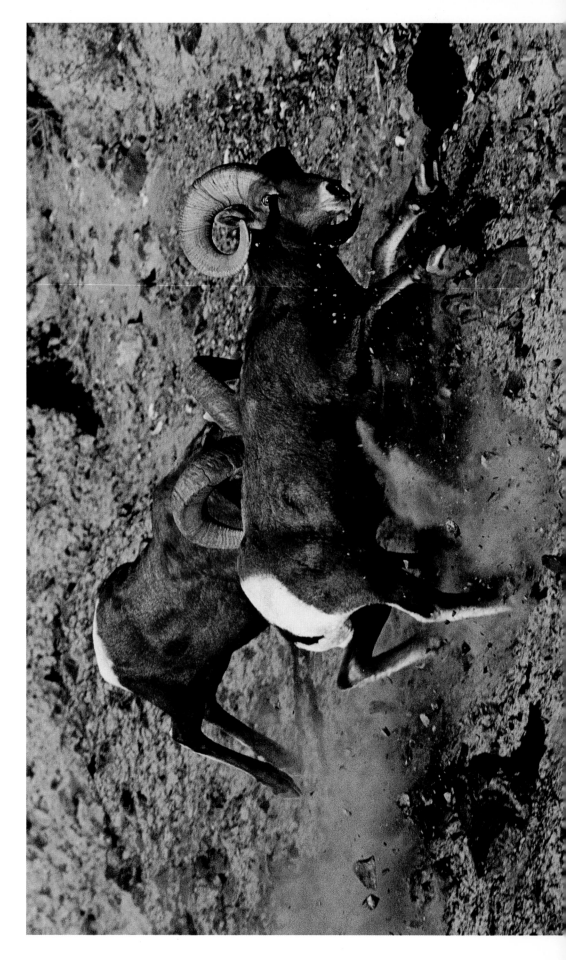

△ △ *Bighorn rams spar for the right to breed at Hart Mountain National Antelope Refuge (Oregon). The full-curved horns of the mature males are "broomed" off on the ends, evidence of many years of fighting and hard survival. Despite these challenges, Hart Mountain bighorn sheep are so productive they are routinely captured and relocated. Refuge bighorns are playing a vital role in repopulating historic bighorn sheep throughout the northwest. Though they may look similar, this species is the California bighorn, which has evolved differently than its desert cousins.*
△ *The desert is filled with sharp edges and prickly thorns. Poised atop a prickly pear pad, a dainty Harris antelope squirrel removes a cactus needle from its paw.* △ *Nestled in an embrace of thorns, the buckhorn cholla's flowers are beautiful, but ephemeral.*

119

△ A jackrabbit could not outrun the golden eagle, which can spot him from a mile away and swoop at speeds of up to 150 miles per hour. Rare in the East, the golden eagle is common at refuges throughout the western United States. △ A young prairie rattlesnake suns itself, unbothered by the thorns of the prickly pear cactus. ▷ Even though it is located in one of the most arid regions of the country, hidden caches of water persist at Kofa National Wildlife Refuge (Arizona), enough for a small fellow like the red-spotted toad. The wary amphibian is never far from a crevice wide enough to serve as a hiding place. Kofa is an acronym for King of Arizona, a gold mine in the region that was active in the 1880s.

Northern Shores & Tundra

The Aleut Eskimos call it Alyeska, the "great land." It is a place with highland glaciers the size of small states and hissing volcanoes that fume and rumble within the Pacific Ocean's Ring of Fire. Serrated mountain ranges jab the sky. Huge lakes and braided rivers hundreds of miles long scribe the landscape. Craggy rocks, spires, and islands by the thousands extend from the coastline. There are infinite horizons, coupled with awesome beauty and friendly isolation. It is a symbolic landscape, where the nation's largest wilderness areas sustain a legacy of plants, animals, and wildness that nourish our souls and our dreams.

If superimposed upon a map of the Lower 48 states, Alaska would stretch from San Diego to Savannah. This great land also sustains wildlife on a grand scale: the largest grizzly bears in the world, the most bald eagles, hundreds of thousands of caribou, millions of spawning salmon, tens of millions of nesting seabirds, billions of fierce mosquitoes.

Alaska national wildlife refuge lands could fill half of Texas. The Arctic and Yukon Delta National Wildlife Refuges are bigger

△ *Caribou traverse the arctic plain, a scene that conveys the grandeur and rugged isolation of Alaska's sixteen national wildlife refuges. Alaska's refuges encompass seventy-six million acres, about 85 percent of the land protected within the National Wildlife Refuge System.*

than many states. Even the smallest Alaskan refuge, Selawik, is larger than most refuges in the Lower 48. Together Alaska refuges account for more than seventy-six million acres, almost 85 percent of land in the National Wildlife Refuge System. Only two refuges have roads. About 20 percent of all refuge lands are designated wildernesses, and much of this vast acreage is protected on Alaskan refuges.

Alaska animals and plants are superbly adapted to the rigors of an unforgiving environment and the seasonal pulses of nature's bounty. On the North Slope and coastal plain of the Arctic National Wildlife Refuge, winter lasts nine months and brings a scant eight inches of rain. The sea churns with jagged ice floes and the stabbing wind sweeps over the austere tundra landscape. Yet caribou, Dall sheep, mountain goats, muskoxen, and all three species of American bears survive on the refuge during winter, finding vegetation protected in rock crevices, beneath the sheltered snow of the taiga (boreal forest), or in wind-blown clearings. Miles of unbroken forest soften the impact of storms, providing winter shelter for the wolf, lynx, snowshoe hare, and others.

During spring and summer, warm weather and moisture trapped atop the permafrost below the poorly drained soil transforms dormant seeds into wildflowers, cotton grass, and other vegetation. Roots reach for moisture and tiny petals blaze with color during the short growing season of only three months. Arctic tundra plants survive by hugging the earth, providing a low profile to the harsh, desiccating wind. A century old pine with twisted branches may be barely twenty feet tall. The fragile land revives slowly; plants can take a decade to reappear and the scars of old trails may remain for centuries. But for a brief few months, the plain and taiga teem with life. Polar bears emerge from winter dens with their cubs. Muskox give birth, and caribou make long journeys to the coastal plain to calve. Snow geese, ducks, and shorebirds stock up on nutritious food before migrating south to breed. At least fifty species of song-birds breed in the taiga.

Rain is scarce in the eastern Arctic tundra, while lush western pine forests on islands at Alaska Maritime and Alaska Peninsula National Wildlife Refuges may receive over two hundred inches of rain each year, more than the Amazon jungles. One group of islands is cloaked with old growth forests and grassy meadows. Another offers volcanic mounds capped with tundra or sheer-faced lava pinnacles, spires, and headlands. Whales spout between huge chunks of polar ice and bald eagles cruise overhead. Sea otters loaf in fog-bound bays and Steller sea lions haul out on a few secluded shores. In a place where wind and storm-lashed seas are the norm, some of the world's largest seabird colonies flourish. Most secluded refuge islands rarely see humans. For several decades refuge workers have removed introduced foxes from many islands, bringing safety and a better chance of nesting success to the vulnerable birds. From cliff-side crevices to soil-capped permafrost, these areas also provide diverse nesting conditions. Spires and slopes offer an easy commute to sea, where seabirds can skim the surface or fly under water to catch squid, crustaceans, and other marine edibles. Isolation breeds some rarities, such as high concentrations of ancient murrelets, an unusual population of singing voles, and a lake of landlocked chinook salmon.

Ocean-living salmon normally seek Alaska's streams and rivers, such as the Yukon, Kuskokwim, and Kenai, to spawn. They enter freshwater in staggering numbers at Kenai, Yukon Delta, and Alaska Peninsula/Becharof Refuges and travel hundreds of miles seeking the familiar chemistry of the streamwater where they were born to spawn. Huge gatherings of grizzly bears and bald eagles rely on their rich sustenance, feeding on the living fish and deteriorating carcasses. Other fish feed on the drifting eggs and the stream is enriched with marine nutrients as the salmon decompose. Partially consumed salmon dropped by a bear or eagle provide food for smaller creatures. What remains nourishes the soil as it decomposes, reviving an earth holding so much promise.

Riverside drying racks festooned with bright salmon meat testify to the importance of these returning fish to the diet and culture of many of Alaska's Native peoples. The Aleut, Inupiat, Athabascan, Yupik, and other groups have had a close and enduring bond with the land and its creatures for thousands of years. The Alaska Native Claims Settlement Act passed in 1971 provided Native people with compensation for land that was taken from them. In addition to giving the tribes money and a choice of new land, including that on refuges, the federal law promised to withdraw up to eighty million acres of land to be used for national wildlife refuges, parks, forests, and other preserves. That commitment was honored in the Alaska National Interest Lands Conservation Act of 1980, which created nine new national wildlife refuges and expanded or renamed seven existing refuges, adding more than fifty-two million acres to the Refuge System.

There is some active management on refuges such as prescribed burning, research, and monitoring, but for the most part these vast lands are simply protected. Safeguarding this untarnished bounty also preserves something for people that resonates deeply within the human spirit. There is maiden earth no other has touched; wisdom in ancient rocks and wind-ravaged trees; and bone-deep silence and companionable solitude. These places of refuge are also a touchstone for people, where the great land and its creatures bring understanding, renewal, and hope within reach. ☞

△ *A shaggy muskox browses on spring wildflowers, a knoll masking his bulky body. The Inupiat called muskoxen* umingmak, *the bearded ones, after the long dense skirt of hair hanging below their knees. About thirty years ago, muskoxen were relocated to the North Slope in an effort to bolster their numbers. Their population on Arctic National Wildlife Refuge has increased annually in recent years.*

▽ *Every year millions of salmon fight their way up the Yukon, Kuskokwim, and Kenai Rivers, seeking the streams of their birth to spawn. They change from bright silver to brilliant red, stop eating, and even grow large sharp teeth on their journey. Scores of species rely on salmon for survival, from grayling, trout, and ducks that eat the tender eggs to bears and eagles that snag whole fish. Salmon are also vitally important to Alaska's Native peoples and to the state's recreation industry. Salmon runs of international renown occur at many refuges, including Kodiak, Kenai, Koyukuk, Togiak, Yukon Delta, and Yukon Flats, their longest migration. This coho salmon is making its way home.*

Olaus and Mardy Murie

In the summer of 1921, Margaret (Mardy) Thomas and Olaus Murie, a young scientist from the Bureau of Biological Survey sent to study caribou, joined friends for a boat ride up Moose Creek, near Fairbanks, Alaska. Mardy recalled hearing the call of a great horned owl and Olaus answering, the two hooting until ". . . out of nowhere the dark soft shape floated into a treetop right above us." Later that evening, Olaus sketched the owl, the first of countless illustrations documenting a lifetime of research and shared adventures in the Alaska wilderness.

During their extensive travels on foot, by dog-sled, and in boats, the two discovered a soul-deep love for each other, and of nature, that eventually shaped major legislation, such as the 1964 Wilderness Act, and guided organizations. Olaus went on to become the director, then president, of the Wilderness Society, saving many untrammeled havens from the bulldozer.

In 1948 the couple built a cabin along the Snake River in Wyoming, which became a gathering place for the world's foremost conservationists and scientists. Their final 1956 Alaskan trip to document the rare Arctic wilderness, and continued advocacy, helped to spearhead creation of the Arctic National Wildlife Refuge, which now includes eight million acres of wilderness.

Since Olaus's death in 1963, Mardy has continued to be a voice for the wilderness, reiterating in 1998 the central theme of their lifelong work. "There may be people who feel no need for nature. They are fortunate perhaps. But for those of us who feel otherwise, who feel something is missing unless we can hike across land disturbed only by our footsteps, or see creatures running freely as they have always done, we are sure there should be wilderness." From tiny Pelican Island to the sprawling Arctic, sixty-six national wildlife refuges today protect more than twenty million acres of designated wilderness.

Caribou

No one knows the ways of the wind and caribou," suggests Native American wisdom about stalking this northern nomad. The Arctic caribou survives brutal winter temperatures greater than fifty degrees below zero, its hollow hair providing insulation from knifing winds and stabbing cold. The herd migrates thousands of miles between tundra and taiga, following a route that varies from year to year. Billions of flies and mosquitoes may turn them from the best forage. Raging rivers and deep snows can divert them over windswept ridges. They walk on large, concave hooves that are instruments for travel and foraging. Their name is *xalibu*, originating from the Newfoundland Micmac Indian word for "the animal who paws." Grizzly bears hibernate, snow geese fly south, but caribou remain active throughout the Arctic winter, often journeying to sheltered forests where it is easier to dig for plants beneath the lightly packed snow. With an uncanny instinct, caribou know where to go. Seen from the air, the tattoo of their passage is an indelible web of crossing and meandering trails linking seasons and generations.

There are at least two dozen caribou herds in Alaska and several are on national wildlife refuges. Named for its seasonal crossing of the Porcupine River in both Alaska and Canada, the Porcupine Herd is the third largest at 123,000. This herd is inextricably linked to wilderness and especially, the Arctic coastal plain, where they

△ △ *Gray wolves haunt the fringes of the caribou herd, traveling as much as thirty miles a day to catch an unwary calf or ailing adult.*
△ *True nomads of the north, caribou may wander thousands of miles a year to find food. The herd browses on tiny tundra plants without lingering, which helps spare the fragile, slow-growing vegetation.*

wetlands, river deltas, and uplands. Two of the nation's largest rivers, and a maze of smaller ones, meander past lakes and wetlands on the treeless tundra plain, then spread out and flow into the Bering Sea. Millions of shorebirds nest here; millions of salmon travel hundreds of miles up these rivers to spawn; two herds of caribou pass through the refuge uplands. This is also the nation's main waterfowl nursery, where over a million ducks and a half-million geese return to nest. Most of the tundra swans of the Atlantic and Pacific flyways nest here. Nearly all of North America's emperor and cackling Canada geese also nest, along with huge numbers of white-fronted geese and brant. Aerial surveys in 1984 showed a sharp decline in these four geese. The refuge worked with dozens of Yup'ik villages to halt subsistence hunting, and hunters in Washington, Oregon, and California agreed to similar restrictions. This cooperation, and the protection of breeding grounds on a single national wildlife refuge have made a difference, allowing cackling Canada geese to rebound from 25,000 to 200,000 and Pacific white-fronted geese to increase from 90,000 to more than 400,000.

Pilot biologists also stay busy on the Yukon Flats in interior Alaska. More than a half dozen rivers, and over twenty thousand lakes and ponds in a pristine setting make this perhaps the world's greatest duck factory, especially when drought occurs in the prairie pothole states and provinces. Often more than one and a half million waterfowl breed here, the highest density of nesting ducks in Alaska. Millions of waterfowl also stop over in fall.

This bounty was nearly destroyed in 1959, when a dam was proposed to create a reservoir the size of Lake Erie, so large it would require twenty years to fill. In a scramble to halt the Rampart Dam, several agencies joined forces to survey the area's main wildlife resources. With barely three years to complete the work, Fish and Wildlife Service pilots in float-planes confirmed a conservative estimate of a million and a half nesting waterfowl, and hopscotched from lake to lake, setting up mobile camps to band waterfowl. By the mid 1960s more than forty thousand ducks were banded. The fate of a continent's waterfowl legacy fired the hearts and imaginations of waterfowl supporters from around the globe, who responded with such force that the dam proposal was dropped. Ever greater waterfowl numbers were documented

over the following years, which in 1978 formed the basis for establishing the 8.6-million-acre Yukon Flats National Wildlife Refuge, and later, six others that protect vital waterfowl habitat.

At all of Alaska's sixteen national wildlife refuges each summer, courtship dances and breeding have produced another generation of fuzzy-headed youngsters that have grown and learned to fly. On frosty fall days, millions of ducks, geese, and swans depart for milder climes. Some will pound the sky with steady wing beats at speeds of forty to sixty miles per hour. Others may cover up to three thousand miles in thirty days. Many will fight squalls that sap their strength and blow them off course. Each flies a time-honed route charted by other seasoned travelers to a destination offering a respite from the savage winter, food to build up fat reserves, and a place to begin their courtship the following spring. For many, that place is another national wildlife refuge. ☛

▽ A pair of Barrow's goldeneyes is easy to see and identify from the ground. Each spring, Fish and Wildlife Service pilot biologists fly designated routes in specially equipped planes to count ducks for the North American waterfowl breeding census. "On nesting surveys you're flying about 150 feet above the ground," observes Alaskan pilot Bruce Conant. "You're looking at habitats where you'd expect to see certain species. You're also looking from above for a rump mark or wing patch, a specific silhouette, or other identifying marks to determine the breed and sex. You're doing all this at ninety-six miles per hour, so the experience is like speed-reading, with impressions gathered in quick glimpses."

△ *More than 220,000 lesser sandhill cranes leave Texas, parts of the Southwest, and the Pacific Coast to breed in Alaska. Most of the midcontinent cranes pass through Tetlin National Wildlife Refuge, fanning out to perform their courtship dances and breed. This crane has selected an island in a beaver pond for her nest.*

NORTHERN SHORES & TUNDRA

STELLER SEA LION

Big and tawny-colored with a shaggy mane like an African lion's, the Steller sea lion's stature or prowess on the sea have not kept them safe. Unlike fur seals, Steller sea lions escaped slaughter because they lacked their cousin's highly coveted fur. The muscular marine mammals hauled out and gave birth to their dark-colored pups in rookeries from Russia to Japan and Alaska south to California, where they thrived. In the 1970s there were about 280,000 Steller sea lions worldwide.

By the mid 1980s, Alaska's western population had declined by 50 percent and portions have since plummeted by 85 percent. They weren't overhunted. The adults appeared to be healthy. Competition for prey with commercial fishing was suspected. The loss was so precipitous that the western populations were declared endangered in 1990.

Critical habitat has been designated and no fishing zones have been established, but the losses continued. Research points to a low birth rate, a low survival rate among the young, and perhaps nutritional stress. Predation by orcas, entrapment in fishing nets or by trawlers, and other causes are also being considered. Most of the seals sea lions haul out and breed on Alaska Maritime National Wildlife Refuge, which coordinates with the National Marine Fisheries Service and particularly, the National Marine Mammal Laboratory, on research, surveys, and other management issues.

△ *The Steller sea lion spends most of its life at sea but breeds on secluded beaches and rocky areas. It was named for Wilhelm Steller who, in 1741, was first to describe its otterlike face, ability to move across land, and formidable lionlike roar.*

△ A bald eagle nest perched on a pinnacle has a penthouse view of the Gulf of Alaska and Kodiak National Wildlife Refuge. This sea-battered terrain is a world unto itself, encompassing rugged mountains, sweeping shorelines, dense forests, huge lakes, and more than a dozen rivers. True to Alaska's reputation for grandeur, some of the world's legendary salmon runs and its biggest brown bears inhabit the island, along with a million and a half seabirds and the largest gathering of nesting bald eagles in the United States.

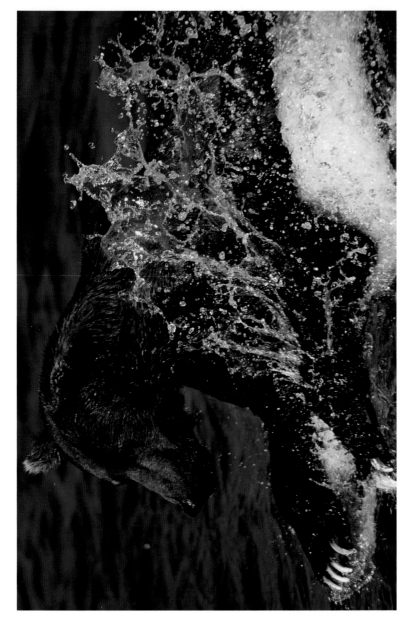

△ Grizzly bears are little more than a memory in most of the Lower 48 states, but they thrive in Alaska. Those that live along the coast are called coastal brown bears, while their inland cousins are known as grizzlies. They can stand upright and use their paws almost as hands; no wonder the Tlinglit think of brown bears as half human and the Inuit suspect they can leave their heavy fur and walk like a man. Hundreds of coastal brown bears fish the salmon streams surrounding Becharof Lake within the Becharof National Wildlife Refuge, forming one of the highest concentrations of brown bears in the United States. ▽ Five species of salmon leave the Bering Sea when they are two to four years old to follow five major rivers into the heart of Togiak National Wildlife Refuge. Among the most coveted is the sockeye salmon. Almost all of the sockeyes spawn far inland, above Togiak Lake. △△ Sun and shadow define the raw power of the Kodiak brown bear, which thrives at a national wildlife refuge devoted to its care.

Barely a pound at birth, the Kodiak brown bear

may tower over nine feet

and weigh fifteen hundred pounds in its prime.

Coastal
Brown Bear

On the north edge of the Pacific Rim tides bathe and storms batter a string of islands, reefs, and seamounts isolated from mainland Alaska by distance and time. It is a scenic, unspoiled wilderness surrounded by one of the most biologically productive ecosystems in the world. The centerpiece is Kodiak, a one-hundred-mile-long island skirted by rugged coastline and offshore rocks used by two million seabirds. Its chiseled mountains and hidden valleys shelter red fox and introduced Sitka black-tailed deer. Pristine lakes and rivers support five species of spawning salmon. It is also home to a unique race of giants.

Barely a pound at birth, the Kodiak brown bear may tower over nine feet and weigh fifteen hundred pounds in its prime. Kodiaks are the largest brown bears, or grizzlies, in the world. They gain their great stature from the island's incredible diversity, where twelve thousand years of separation from the mainland have made these bears genetically distinct. Those in the mountain valleys feast on lush grasses, sedges, and abundant berries. They congregate along prolific salmon streams and lakes, some supporting two hundred feeding bears, a density seldom matched around the world. On rocky southern beaches, bears devour insects hiding in kelp or marine mammal carcasses that have washed ashore. Kodiak bears flourish here and throughout the archipelago, consuming eighty to ninety pounds of food per day to prepare for winter and the birth of their cubs during hibernation. Management has involved studying the bears' food preferences, movements, and population densities; learning how deer hunting and public viewing affect them; and assuring that this unique setting is protected.

Three presidents have recognized the national value of the bears and their wilderness domain. In 1892, Benjamin

The Fish and Wildlife Service made purchase of these Native inholdings their top acquisition priority. But in the days following the oil spill, negotiations halted as worried Kodiak residents and refuge staff saw gooey mousse from the spill become trapped in their bays and blanket their shorelines. Marine life was decimated, a huge blow for commercial fishermen, including the Alutiiq, who earned as much as twenty million dollars annually from the Karluk and Sturgeon river salmon. As they watched their livelihoods and legacies destroyed, recreation-based development of their inholdings seemed inevitable.

The Kodiak Brown Bear Trust, a conservation group representing national interests in conserving the brown bear and its habitat in a manner sensitive to the Alutiiq, has helped keep the partners talking. Negotiations were made public, the State and refuge embarked on a bear management plan, and citizen advisory committees were established, which helped to create an unprecedented level of public participation that has since become a model for the nation. Parties have worked to set aside distrust. Their common ground has been the refuge and what is best for the brown bear.

The results are also without precedent. Willing Native corporations have sold inholdings or negotiated conservation easements to the Fish and Wildlife Service to return 276,000 acres to refuge management. The purchases have been made with $150,000,000 from the oil spill, and government and private funds, representing the largest addition to an existing refuge, through acquisition, in the history of the Refuge System. Public use of the Karluk Lake inholdings are being managed by the refuge under a multiyear conservation easement that could lead to full acquisition.

To the Alutiiq, the mere presence of the brown bear evokes fear and inspires awe. So powerful is his totem that they do not refer to him by name. He is the brown one, the big-footed one, the great one. His meat has given sustenance, his shaggy coat has provided warmth, his teeth are proudly worn, his bone and sinew the source of tools. He is the backbone of a culture, an economy, and the giver and taker of life. The Kodiak brown bear is an icon, symbolic of all that is wild and a partnership forged of necessity to preserve a giant, a refuge large enough to sustain him, and the First People's right to a way of life. ⌐

Harrison set aside neighboring Afognak Island as a Forest and Fish Culture Reserve, in 1907 President Theodore Roosevelt established Afognak as part of the Chugach National Forest, and in 1941, Franklin Roosevelt made two-thirds of Kodiak Island a national wildlife refuge for the brown bear. The lives of its brown bears, millions of spawning salmon, and the Alutiiq or "First People," who have lived on the island for 7,500 years, are geographically and culturally intertwined. They are also bound by legislation and the March 1989 *Exxon Valdez* oil spill, when the supertanker leaked eleven million gallons of oil, some of which was carried by wind and tides to pristine Kodiak. Through the efforts of a partnership led by the refuge, state of Alaska, Alutiiq people, Kodiak Brown Bear Trust, and others, the environmental tragedy surrounding the refuge was turned into one of the most compelling conservation successes of the century.

The refuge and its brown bears were the focal point of discussions beginning in 1971, when the Alaska Native Claims Settlement Act fulfilled a promise made to its Native people in 1959, upon Alaska's statehood, to return control of their historic lands. On Kodiak, the Native corporations

selected 310,000 acres of prime forest, river, and coastal habitats within the refuge. This included several vital bear feeding areas, including the rich Karluk Lake watershed, which holds three times more salmon than the 2,500 watersheds of Oregon's Columbia River. A special provision of the law forbade the Kodiak corporations from selling their land to any non-Native for twenty years, directed them to give the government the first right to purchase land, and required them to manage it without interfering with brown bears and refuge regulations. For the Alutiiq, encumbering their land with these requirements devalued what they had waited a century to receive and gave them little recourse. These lands had no oil fields, timber, or mines to develop. To create a livelihood and preserve their way of life, the Alutiiq considered building roads and resorts, renting hunting and fishing lodges, and developing tourism, which would surely conflict with refuge purposes and regulations. To protect the national interest, the Alutiiq's cultural and economic interests, and preserve a wealth of wild salmon, wild bears, and wild country, a win-win solution was essential between parties with a history of distrust.

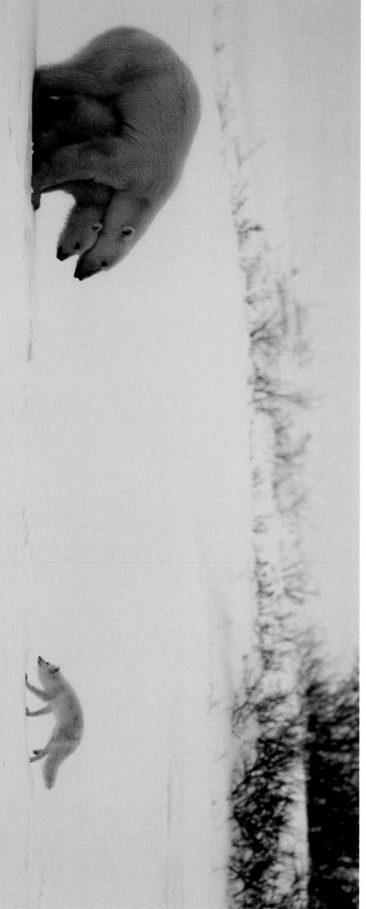

△ *Most Alaska refuges are very remote and secluded, but Kenai National Wildlife Refuge is only a three-hour drive from Anchorage, drawing more than 300,000 visitors annually. Easy access and the lure of trophy moose caused Kenai Peninsula moose numbers to plummet. Weeks after the 1941 bombing of Pearl Harbor, President Franklin Roosevelt established the Kenai National Moose Range. The area became a national wildlife refuge in 1980, protecting such a wealth of habitat and wildlife diversity that the refuge is sometimes considered Alaska in miniature.*

▷ *Long-tailed ducks, also called Oldsquaws, are known for their long black tails and nonstop chatter. They winter on both the Atlantic and Pacific Coasts, but return to Alaska to breed on secluded tundra ponds, such as those protected at Arctic National Wildlife Refuge.*

▽ *A polar mother assumes a defensive posture as an opportunistic arctic fox moves in to scavenge what the bear leaves behind. The ice bear, or sea bear as it is sometimes called, is well adapted to life in the frigid arctic marine environment. Dense fur and blubber keep it warm. Sharp, curved claws and tiny projections on the soles of each foot give better traction on the ice. Webbed toes and oar-shaped feet make it a good swimmer. Polar bears live at the edge of the floating ice pack, some traveling up to three thousand miles each year. Though they look and live much differently than brown bears, they are from the same stock, one adapting to land, and the other, to the sea.*

ACKNOWLEDGMENTS

America's Wildlife Refuges has been a caring collaboration that spans the entire nation. Our heartfelt appreciation is extended to Rick Coleman, former Chief of the National Wildlife Refuge System and current Chief of Refuges/Mountain Prairie Region; Kevin Kilcullen, Branch Chief for Visitor Services; and Susan Saul, Outreach Specialist/Pacific Region, for their vision, their enthusiastic and enduring support, and for championing *America's Wildlife Refuges* within the Fish and Wildlife Service. We offer special thanks to our publishers, Carpe Diem Books® and Graphic Arts Center Publishing Company, for their perseverance in shepherding this project through its many phases. We are grateful to Ross Eberman, Tim Frew, Kirsten Leonard, and Jean Andrews—the project team—for their patience and flexibility, and for welcoming our participation in the design process.

Tom gives special recognition to his friend and fellow wildlife photographer, Tom Kitchin, for sharing the adventure and expenses of the weeks spent at Arctic National Wildlife Refuge. He and Pat also appreciate Arscentia (formerly Wy'east Color) for reducing film development fees on the 1,700 rolls of film used for this project.

Jeanne warmly recognizes her husband, Bill, a retired Fish and Game wildlife biologist, for sharing years of firsthand wildlife field experiences with her, for his thoughtful reviews of the manuscript, and for his steady love and belief in her.

Along the way, nearly two hundred Fish and Wildlife Service employees gave generously of their time and talent to shape and review the book. They welcomed the Leesons and Stones to their refuges, often taking them to the best settings for capturing beautiful images of scenery and wildlife. They warmly responded to Jeanne's visits, telephone calls, and e-mails. They made suggestions regarding species and stories to consider; provided reference materials and suggested other people to contact; gave knowledgeable and patient interviews; and/or carefully reviewed their portions of the manuscript. A book of this scope would have been impossible without their support. Often people helped, but gave only a first name; our apologies are extended to those we did not list.

INTRODUCTION

Agassiz: Gary Tischer; **Bear River:** Karen Lindsey; **Hakalau Forest:** Dick Wass; **Turnbull:** Sandy Rancourt; **Upper Mississippi River:** Eric Nelson; **Mountain Prairie Region/Chief of Refuges:** Rick Coleman; **National Conservation Training Center:** David Klinger; **Pacific Region Office/External Affairs:** Susan Saul.

CONTINENTAL WETLANDS

Aransas: Dr. David Blankinship, Tom Stehn; **Brazoria/San Bernard:** Mike Lange; **Chassahowitzka:** Takaka Hashimoto; **Chataugua:** Ron Fischer; **Forsythe:** Jorge Coppen; **Horicon:** Diane Bentelow; **Karl Mundt:** Gene Williams; **Klamath:** Jim Heinlein, Dave Mauser, Dave Menke; **J. Clark Salyer:** Gary Erickson; **Patuxent:** Ray Erickson (retired), Kathleen O'Malley, B. H. Powell; **Sacramento:** Denise Dachner, Greg Mensik, Mike Wolder; **Sand Lake:** William Schultze; **San Luis:** Kim Forrest, John Fulton, Gary Zahm (retired); **Sequoyah:** Craig Hefflebower; **Southeast Louisiana Refuges:** Nancy Walters; **Stillwater:** Janet Schmidt, Donna Withers; **Sonny Bono Salton Sea:** Jihadda Govan, Sylvia Pelizza; **California DFG:** John Fischer; **G. M. Sutton Avian Research Center:** M. Alan Jenkins; **Hawk Mountain:** Keith Bildstein, **Idaho Fish and Game:** Terry Mansfield; **Mountain Prairie Regional Office:** Ron Reynolds; **Pacific Region/California Nevada Office:** Dave Paullin; **Pacific Region/Migratory Bird Program:** Mike Green, Ralph Opp (retired Oregon DFG).

ISLANDS AND BEACHES

Alaska Maritime: Vernon Byrd; **Archie Carr:** Paul Tritaik; **Bombay Hook:** Frank Smith; **Don Edwards San Francisco Bay/Farallon:** Joelle Buffa; **Hawaiian Islands:** Steve Barclay, Beth Flint, Rod Shallenberger (retired FWS); **Kilauea Point:** Dave Aplin, Kathy Batha; **Monomoy:** Sharon Marino; **Oregon Coast/Three Arch Rocks:** Roy Lowe; **Petit Manan:** Linda Welch; **Yukon Delta:** Brian McCaffrey, Michael Rearden; **Maine Fish and Wildlife:** Brad Allen; **Marine Endeavors:** Mark Rauzon; **Pacific Islands Ecoregion Office:** Ann Bell; **Alaska Regional Office:** Russ Oates; **Washington D.C. Migratory Bird Office:** Brad Andres.

WESTERN MOUNTAINS AND PLAINS

Atwater Prairie Chicken: Nancy Morrissey, Terry Rossignol; **Benton Lake:** Bob F. Johnson; **Bosque del Apache:** John Taylor; **Bowdoin:** Valerie Kopesco; **Charles M. Russell:** Randy Matchett; **Des Lacs:** Dan Severson; **Grays Lake:** Carl Mitchell; **Lostwood:** Brad Andres, Fred Giese; **Mississippi Sandhill Crane:** Jim Kurth, Scott Hereford; **Neal Smith:** Pauline Drobney, Nancy Gilbertson; **National Bison:** Pat Jamieson, Lindy Garner, Dave Wiseman; **Red Rock Lakes:** Danny Gomez, Carl Mitchell; **San Bernard:** Mike Lange; **Seney/Kirtlands Warbler:** Mike Tansy; **Stone Lakes:** Tom Harvey; **Wichita:** Joe Kimball; **Yukon Delta:** Brian McCaffrey; **Arizona Game and Fish:** Frosty Taylor; **Bismark Field Office:** Ron Reynolds; **Clemson University:** Sidney A. Gauthreaux; **Northern Prairie Research Center:** Gary Krapu; **Mountain Prairie Region/Partners in Flight:** Terry Rich.

SOUTHERN SHORES AND SWAMPS

Alligator River/Red Wolf Recovery Team: Shauna Baron; **Big Boggy:** Mike Lange; **Arthur R. Marshall Loxahatchee:** Marion Bailey, Dr. Laura Brandt; **Chassahowitzka:** Joyce Kleen, Jim Kraus; **Cedar Keys:** Steve Barlow; **Chase Lake:** Mike Erickson; **Crystal River:** Shawn Gillette; **Lacassine:** Stan Howater; **Florida Panther National Wildlife Refuge:** Layne Hamilton; **Mandalay:** Steve Reagan; **National Key Deer:** Dr. Phil Frank; **Okefenokee:** Sara Aicher, Cindy Thompson; **Ottawa:** Ron Huffman; **Pelican Island:** Paul Tritaik; **Tensas:** Jerome Ford; **Audubon:** Emilie Payne (volunteer); **Southwest Region/Ecological Services:** Robyn Cobb, Phil Glass; **University of California/Davis:** Dan Anderson.

AMERICAN DESERTS

Ash Meadows: Eric Hopsen; **Cabeza Prieta:** John Morgart; **Desert:** Clay Courtright, Bruce Zeller; **Kofa:** Ray Varney; **Sevillita:** Kimberly King-Wrenn; **Sheldon/Hart:** Mike Dunbar, Mike Nunn, Gale Monson (FWS retired).

NORTHERN SHORES AND TUNDRA

Alaska Maritime: Poppy Benson, Vernon Byrd; **Alaska Peninsula/Becharof:** Susan Savage; **Arctic:** Alan Brackney, Steve Kendall, Ed Mallek, Fran Mauer (now retired); **Izembek:** Kristine Sowl; **Kanuti:** Lisa Saperstein; **Kodiak:** Leslie Kerr, Bill Pyle; **Koyukuk:** Mike Spindler; **San Joaquin:** Dennis Woolington; **San Luis:** Kim Forrest; **Yukon Delta:** Dave Cannon, Steve Kovach, Brian McCaffrey, Chris Harwood, Mike Rearden, Mike Wege, Cynthia Wentworth; **Yukon Flats:** Mark Bertram, Ted Heuer, Jim King; **Regional Office:** Dr. Patrica Heglund, Russ Oates, Dave Patterson, Dave Payer, Steven Shuck, Bruce Woods, Tony Chatto (FWS retired); **Juneau Field Office:** Bruce Conant; **Aleutian Canada Goose Recovery Team:** Forrest Lee (FWS retired), Dr. Paul Springer (University of California/Humboldt); **Alutiiq Museum:** Sven Haakanson; **California DFG:** Dan Yparraguirre; **Kodiak Brown Bear Trust:** David Cline (former FWS).

OTHER FISH AND WILDLIFE SERVICES

Assistant Chief of Refuges: Jim Kurth; **Fish and Wildlife Service Historian:** Mark Madison; **Migratory Birds/Flyway Coordinators:** George T. Allen, Brad Andrus, Tim Moser, Jerry Serie, Dave Sharp, John Trapp, Robert Trost; **Montezuma:** Tom Jasikoff; **Natural Resources/Wilderness:** Nancy Roeper; **Non Game Bird Coordinators:** Scott Flaherty, Bill Howe, Stephanie Jones, Ken Rosenberg; **Partners in Flight Program:** Carol Beardmore, Terry Rich, Steve Lewis; **Refuges Webmaster:** Sandra Hodala; **Wetlands Program:** Bill Willen; **Pacific Region:** Kirk Lambert; **Southwest Region:** Juli Niemann, Jeannie WagnerGreven; **Great Lakes/Big Rivers Region:** Don Hultman, Jon Kauffeld, Jim Leach, Chuck Traxler; **Northeast Region:** Bill Laskowski, Jan D. Taylor; **Mountain Prairie Region:** Diane Emmons.

OTHERS

Audubon Society: Pete Dunne, Gretchen Muller; **California Waterfowl Association:** Becky Easter; **National Wildlife Refuge Association:** Evan Hirsche; **Peregrine Fund:** Bill Henrich; **The Nature Conservancy:** Mike Dennis, Steven J. McCormick; **Support and Review:** Carol Field, Bill Grenfell (retired California DFG), and Dennis Lewon.

NATIONAL WILDLIFE REFUGE OFFICES

Washington, D.C. Office
U.S. Fish and Wildlife Service
1849 C. Street, N.W.
Washington, D.C. 20240
www.fws.gov

Pacific Region (1)
U.S. Fish and Wildlife Service
911 N.E. Eleventh Avenue
Portland, OR 97232-4181
[CA, ID, HI, NV, OR, WA, Guam, American Samoa]
http://pacific.fws.gov

Southwest Region (2)
U.S. Fish and Wildlife Service
500 Gold Avenue, S.W., Room 3018
P.O. Box 1306
Albuquerque, NM 87103-1306
[AZ, NM, OK, TX]
http://southwest.fws.gov

Great Lakes-Big Rivers Region (3)
U.S. Fish and Wildlife Service
1 Federal Drive
BHW Federal Building
Fort Snelling, MN 55111-4056
[IL, IN, IA, MI, MN, MO, OH, WI]
http://midwest.fws.gov

Southeast Region (4)
U.S. Fish and Wildlife Service
1875 Century Blvd.
Atlanta, GA 30345-3203
[AR, AL, FL, GA, KY, LA, MS, NC, SC, TN, Puerto Rico]
http://southeast.fws.gov

Northeast Region (5)
U.S. Fish and Wildlife Service
300 Westgate Center Drive
Hadley, MA 01035-9589
[CT, DE, ME, MD, MA, NH, NJ, NY, PA, RI, VT, VA, WV]
http://northeast.fws.gov

Mountain-Prairie Region (6)
U.S. Fish and Wildlife Service
Box 25486 Denver Federal Center
Denver, CO 80225
[CO, KS, MT, NE, ND, SD, UT, WY]
http://mountain-prairie.fws.gov

Alaska Region (7)
1011 East Tudor Road
Anchorage, AK 99503
[AK]
http://alaska.fws.gov

NATIONAL WILDLIFE REFUGE SYSTEM VISITOR GUIDE

Request a free copy of this map and listing of refuges with public access programs. The full-color publications gives seasonal access information and lists the types of public programs and facilities that are available at refuges that allow public access. Almost three hundred refuges have hunting and fishing programs. Most have viewing or education programs. Contact a regional office to request a copy, or call 1 800/344-WILD.

OTHER NATIONAL WILDLIFE REFUGE SYSTEM BOOKS

Butcher, Russell D., *America's National Wildlife Refuges: A Complete Guide*, Roberts Rinehart Publisher, 2003.

Dolin, Eric Jay, *Smithsonian Book of National Wildlife Refuges*, Washington and London, Smithsonian Institution Press, 2003.

Gibson, Daniel, *Audubon Guide to the National Wildlife Refuges: Southwest*, New York, A Balliett and Fitzgerald, Inc. book by St. Martin's Griffin, 2000.

Gove, Doris, *Audubon Guide to the National Wildlife Refuges: Southeast*, New York, A Balliett and Fitzgerald, Inc. book by St. Martin's Griffin, 2000.

Grassy, John, *Audubon Guide to the National Wildlife Refuges: Rocky Mountains*, New York, A Balliett and Fitzgerald, Inc. book by St. Martin's Griffin, 2000.

Grassy, John and Powers, Tom, *Audubon Guide to the National Wildlife Refuges: Northern Midwest*, New York, A Balliett and Fitzgerald, Inc. book by St. Martin's Griffin, 2000.

Laubach, René, *Audubon Guide to the National Wildlife Refuges: New England*, New York, A Balliett and Fitzgerald, Inc. book by St. Martin's Griffin, 2000.

Laycock, George, *The Sign of the Flying Goose: The Story of our National Wildlife Refuges*, New York, Anchor Press/Doubleday, 1973.

MacArthur, Loren, *Audubon Guide to the National Wildlife Refuges: California & Hawaii*, New York, A Balliett and Fitzgerald, Inc. book by St. Martin's Griffin, 2000.

MacArthur, Loren and Miller, Debbie S., *Audubon Guide to the National Wildlife Refuges: Alaska and the Northwest*, New York, A Balliett and Fitzgerald, Inc. book by St. Martin's Griffin, 2000.

Palmer, William, *Audubon Guide to the National Wildlife Refuges: South Central*, New York, A Balliett and Fitzgerald, Inc. book by St. Martin's Griffin, 2000.

Ricciuti, Edward R., *Audubon Guide to the National Wildlife Refuges: Mid-Atlantic*, New York, A Balliett and Fitzgerald, Inc. book by St. Martin's Griffin, 2000.

Riley, Laura and William, *Audubon Guide to the National Wildlife Refuges, United States*, MacMillan General Reference: A Simon & Schuster MacMillan Company, 1979.

PHOTO CREDITS

All photographs are © MMIII by Tom and Pat Leeson except the following, which are listed by page number:

Pages 8, 9, 10,15, 20–21, 39, 43 (top and bottom), 44, 45, 49, 50, 51 (top and bottom), 54, 55 (both), 56 (left), 58, 67 (bottom), 84–85, 88, 90 (top and bottom), 94 (top), 100, 101 (top and bottom), 102, 105, 106–107, 108, 109, 112, 113, 114, 115, 117, 119 (bottom), 120, 121, and back cover are © MMIII by Jason Stone and Gene Stone.

Pages 116 and 123 (bottom) are © MMIII by Jody Stone.